CO▬▬▬▬▬▬
KNOWLEDGE
for the Community College Student

DAVID SCHOEM
University of Michigan

LYNN DUNLAP
Skagit Valley College

Ann Arbor
THE UNIVERSITY OF MICHIGAN PRESS

2014   2013   2012   2011   4   3   2   1

ISBN-13: 978-0-472-03455-0

Library of Congress Cataloging-in-Publication Data

Schoem, David Louis.
    College knowledge for the community college student / David Schoem, Lynn
Dunlap.
        p.   cm.
    ISBN 978-0-472-03455-0 (pbk. : alk. paper)   1.   Community colleges—United
States.   2.   College student orientation—United States.   I.   Dunlap, Lynn.   II.
Title.
    LB2343.32.S34 2011
    378.1'98—dc22

                                                              2010040233

For Our Students

Preface

We have written this book to support the academic success of each and every community college student. This book is written for the community college student for use in class, during orientation, in advance of attending community college, as a pocket guide to carry throughout one's studies at the community college, and/or as a book to rely on for specific help and suggestions and for more general reflection, growth, and support. We hope that community college instructors and administrators will encourage their students to read the book carefully and learn from all the tips.

Each of the tips is grounded in an extensive and substantive body of research about success in college as well as our own extensive experience and the wisdom and advice of our students. We recognize and celebrate the diversity of both community college students and the community colleges themselves. We have attempted to address the wide range of students who attend community colleges as well as the variation in size, structure, practice, demographics, and culture of different community colleges. In keeping with this diversity within and across colleges, we also acknowledge the variety of terms that are used to describe the teachers at community colleges (like *faculty, instructor, professor, teacher*); we elected, for the sake of consistency and simplicity (with a few exceptions), to use the term *instructor* for this position.

A college education is the key to a student's individual future and to our common, collective future. College is an intellectual adventure, an avenue to advancement, and a chance to improve lives. The United States needs well-educated citizens who can think critically and creatively, participate actively, and provide leadership for a strong democracy. We also need innovators in the workplace, producing and inventing a healthy and sustainable future for our children and grandchildren. We need people prepared to listen, dialogue, work, and communicate across our diverse racial, ethnic, economic, and global boundaries and borders. We need loving and caring adults, children, parents, partners, friends, and mentors in our cities and communities.

Lynn Dunlap, who is a first-generation college student, considers herself very fortunate to have taught at community colleges for 30 years. Although she has encountered people who think of community colleges as being in some way "less" than universities—less prestigious, less academically challenging, less socially enriching—her experiences and those of her colleagues at other community colleges around the country suggest the exact opposite, that everything about the community college speaks to **more and better**. Her classes are smaller, she can focus primarily on teaching, and her students are remarkable. The promise of college and its pathway to improving lives is her hope for her students just as it was the hope that her parents held out for her and her sisters and brothers when they enrolled in college for the first time.

Lynn has been a devoted teacher of composition and literature at community colleges throughout the nation, and she also has served as an advisor at community colleges. For most of her professional life she has taught at Skagit Valley College, a community college in Washington. At Skagit Valley College, she coordinated the first years of their innovative General Education program.

Lynn was one of the early national leaders in the area of learning communities and integrated learning, and she has for many years worked closely with the Washington Center for Improving the Quality of Undergraduate Education on the development of effective teaching practices that engage students and lead to deep and meaningful learning. She has been the direct resource faculty member and consultant there to more than 30 community colleges of different sizes and types across the nation, attending week-long summer institutes. She has also worked at the Washington Center as a research collaborator, author, advisory board member, and as a trainer at state-wide faculty retreats.

Lynn is a much sought-after speaker who travels widely to deliver workshops and presentations for faculty and administrators at community colleges around the country. She has conducted program reviews and led trainings at more than a dozen colleges in California, Florida, Maryland, Massachusetts, Michigan, and Missouri. She has collaborated on research projects with faculty and administrators from Chandler-Gilbert Community College in Arizona, Harper College in Illinois, and Delta College in Michigan. Lynn has helped organize and present in conference panels and workshops with community college colleagues from large urban colleges in Chicago, Dallas, Long Beach, and New York City, as well as from rural colleges and branch campuses. Her more recent focus has been on emerging trends in interdisciplinary assessment, helping developmental students reach college readiness, reforming college teaching, and student success in community college.

David Schoem, who is also a first-generation college student, is the Director of the Michigan Community Scholars Program at the University of Michigan. He has spent his entire career there teaching sociology and mentoring college students as a professor, dean, and vice president for academic and student affairs. As a graduate of a large, public, urban high school, David is deeply committed to the promise of education and an educated public, to educational equity, and to giving back to all of those promising and capable individuals, like the many he attended school with, who either didn't graduate from high school or who never continued their studies beyond high school.

David is a nationally known scholar and administrator of higher education and intergroup relations, and has been on the faculty at the University of Michigan since 1979, teaching in areas of education, diversity and intergroup dialogue, social identity, civic engagement, deliberative democracy and social change, and the American Jewish Community. He has given talks and led seminars with faculty and campus leaders at more than 50 colleges--large and small, private and public, urban and rural—including more than 20 years of involvement with the Washington Center for Improving the Quality of Undergraduate Education and its ground-breaking work bringing together faculty from community colleges with faculty from four-year universities. David has published widely, and this is his ninth book.

Most of our time, commitment, and effort throughout our careers have gone to working directly with college students, as their teacher, advisor, mentor, and friend. We have benefited enormously from our relationships with our students, growing and learning from each outstanding individual we have met. We hope this book in some small way expresses our gratitude for all that they have given us.

Acknowledgments

For more than thirty years we have been fortunate to have students share their academic and personal successes, challenges, and life stories with us. We have been first-hand observers of what helped them learn and grow, excel and graduate. We have also heard and seen which approaches to college have not worked so well. We hope all of our students have learned from their time with us, and we are heartened by the many students who remain in touch with us long after their college experiences. But, just as they have learned from us, we now want to thank all of our students for all that we have learned from them. In writing this book, we pass along their wisdom to future generations of community college students.

We are indebted to Kelly Sippell and Philip Pochoda of the University of Michigan Press for their support and encouragement of this project. While it builds on the success of David's earlier book, *College Knowledge: 101 Tips*, they understood that there were unique issues facing community college students and that this population of students would be best served by a book addressing their specific concerns.

We want to thank our colleagues at the Washington Center for Improving the Quality of Undergraduate Education. Co-Directors Emily Lardner and Gillies Malnarich and, formerly, Barbara Leigh Smith and Jean MacGregor, have not only been great resources but have served to help us build relationships with community college and four-year colleagues across the country. Rachel Singer and Janine Graziano-King of Kingsborough Community College; Joye Hardiman and Sonja Wiedenhaupt of the Evergreen State College; Audrey Wright and Janet Ray of Seattle Central Community College; Barbara Williamson of Spokane Falls Community College; Laurette Foster of Prairie View A&M University; and Maureen Pettitt, Gail Davern, Kathy Larson, Bobbi Ashe, and Lynne Fouquette of Skagit Valley College all offered initial encouragement and ideas for this book.

We are also indebted to colleagues who offered specific feedback as we wrote. Eric Anderson clarified the role of community college counselors and student services and, with Denny Reid, checked the accuracy of portions of the book. Trish Barnes and Ann Zukoski provided invaluable suggestions about what helps students succeed in online courses. Larry Sult and Linda Moore helped think through how best to present some of the ideas; Linda additionally provided invaluable assistance with structure and organization. Students Katie Kozowski and Dan Vlasuk provided detailed feedback from the perspective of community college students. Keeping in mind the very diverse ages and backgrounds of all the other students with whom they have taken classes, they read drafts of the tips,

sometimes multiple versions, and offered thoughtful, critical assessments and suggestions for revisions.

In addition, we thank the readers who provided feedback to the University of Michigan Press from Northern Virginia Community College, Hillsborough Community College, Seminole Community College, Bellevue Community College, and Westchester Community College. We also want to thank other colleagues, including Marcos Cicerone of De Anza College; Phyllis Dawkins of the HBCU Faculty Development Network; Ed Dolan of Bellevue Community College and Harper College; Julia Fogarty of Delta College; Jim Harnish of North Seattle Community College; Maria Hesse of Chandler-Gilbert Community College; Gary Hodge of Collin Community College; Ricardo Leyva-Puebla of Tacoma Community College; Jerri Lindblad of Frederick Community College; Marybeth Mason of Chandler-Gilbert Community College; Bill Moore of the Washington State Board of Technical and Community Colleges; Jacque Mott of Harper College; Louise Pagotto of Kapi'olani Community College; Cheryl Roberts of Chemekata Community College; Leslie Roberts of Miami-Dade College; Edwina Stoll of De Anza College; Ana Torres-Bower of Cerritos College; and Phyllis Van Slyck of LaGuardia Community College.

Finally, we wish to thank our families. Lynn wishes to thank her husband, Terry, for his unwavering support and long evening conversations about the important work of community colleges. She is also thankful to her parents, who, despite not having gone to college, believed in education. Her mother, Laura, who had always wanted to be a teacher, coached the whole family, including, ultimately, Lynn's father, through undergraduate and, in some cases, graduate degrees. Her father, Al, whose college plans were interrupted by World War II, taught her that it's never too late to become a student when, in his late forties, still working and helping raise his family, he enrolled in his first college class.

David wishes to thank his loving family for this, his ninth book. His wife, Karyn, and adult daughters, Adina and Shana, have offered constant encouragement. Karyn has been patient beyond words during this past intensive year of book writing. His father, Gerald, was passionately devoted to higher education, despite his never having received a college degree, and his mother, Sara, now eighty-eight years old, has always represented the most vocal and heartfelt cheering section for every endeavor.

Contents

PART 2: THE FUNDAMENTALS OF COLLEGE SUCCESS

Introduction

This book is for you, the community college student. We *want you* to succeed in order for you to realize your life's hopes and dreams. We *need you* to succeed in order for our country to realize our collective hopes and dreams in our common and interconnected future. The community college holds the great educational promise for each individual and for our entire nation.

Most students, like you, arrive at college not fully aware of just how different the college experience is. In some ways, it is like entering a foreign country with customs and rules that are not always obvious or written out. The intellectual and social expectations, as well as the rules and regulations, are different, and not just different from high school. Even students who have owned their own businesses, retired from military careers, recently immigrated to the United States, or enrolled in school for the first time later in life are often surprised that an important part of the challenge of college is just figuring out how to be successful in college.

While all college students must learn to negotiate the transition to college, there are unique challenges for those who enroll in community colleges. Many community college students work, and many work full-time. Many also have family responsibilities—children, partners, and aging parents. A majority of community college students are the first in their family to enroll in college. For many students from abroad and from the United States, English is not their first language or the language they use at home, and many students at community colleges come to study from countries outside the United States. For all these individuals, there may not be any easy road map or "tour guide" in their own family to help figure out how it all works.

We hope, therefore, that this book will serve as your personal road map and guide for a successful community college experience and education. The suggestions we offer are directed specifically to the kinds of situations that are particular to you, the community college student, even as we recognize that you are all very different and have different goals and lifestyles. While we encourage you to read the book from beginning to end, our experience has been that the most useful guidebook is one that you can return to again and again, at the beginning, middle, or end, whenever you face new or unexpected challenges and opportunities.

As you read this book and the various tips in search of guidance, you will quickly learn that there is great diversity among the students who attend community colleges and also many differences that exist between one college and the next. Even if you are aware of this diversity, you may be surprised by just how diverse the students in your classes are. This rich diversity in terms of age, social and educational background, national origin, first language, and life experience is one of the joys of the community college classroom, and you should take full advantage of it.

In any term, you are likely to find students who are still enrolled in high school, students who have graduated high school in the past year, and students who have been out of high school a decade or more. Some students are tentative about being in community college and are just testing the waters, while others have clearly defined and ambitious goals. Some are returning to college after being away from it for a few years, while some are trying community college after a few terms at a university. Others are choosing to go to a community college for two years to get the basic courses done before transferring to a university as a junior. Some community college students never received a high school degree, while others already have college degrees but need refresher classes before pursuing an advanced degree. Still others have recently immigrated to the United States and, as a result, need to establish credentials or develop skills for a career. Some attend because they have lost jobs and are re-tooling or are changing employment because of an injury, a shift in the economy, or a change in their personal lives.

We have attempted to address all of our tips and suggestions in this book to fit as many students attending community colleges as possible, but on occasion you may find that a specific sentence, example, paragraph, or tip may apply more to one population than another. In those cases, we urge you to keep reading to learn more about what your classmates may be experiencing, and because, most likely, the next sentence or the example might pertain to your particular experience.

In terms of the demographics of your fellow classmates, you may be interested to learn just how diverse the students are who attend community colleges. According to the American Association of Community Colleges (www.aacc.nche.edu/AboutCC/Pages/fastfacts.aspx) at the time of this writing:

- ✓ Nearly 12 million students attend one of the 1,173 community colleges, including 31 Tribal Colleges.

- ✓ 46% of students are age 21 or younger.

- ✓ Of the 54% percent of students over the age of 21, 16% are age 40 or older.

- ✓ Minority students represent 40% of the student body.

- ✓ 42% of community college students are the first generation in their family to attend college.

- ✓ 16% of students are single parents.

- ✓ Of the 40% of students who attend full-time, 21% are employed full-time and 59% part-time.

- ✓ Of the 60% enrolled part-time, 40% work full-time, and 47% work part-time.

Indeed, your community college classmates may include small business owners, military veterans, parents, homemakers, tribal elders, dual-enrolled high school students, as well as future leaders of industry and government. Students in community colleges have grown up speaking a great many different languages, have come to the United States from many different countries, and are from many racial and ethnic groups. They come from many different economic backgrounds, and they practice many different religions. They all have in common the desire to learn, grow, improve, and enrich their own lives and their communities.

While there is great diversity in the overall student population attending community colleges, the demographics of the student body at your college may be quite different from the national averages. Please note: The figures on pages 5–7 represent the most recent data posted on college websites at the time that this book went to press. For instance, of the approximately 17,000 students at LaGuardia Community College in New York City in 2010—just to pick one community college--46 percent came from the United States and 54 percent were born in another country (from more than 160 countries). Fifty-nine percent are female, and 41 percent are male. Of those students identifying their race and ethnicity, 36 percent are Hispanic, 18 percent Asian, 15 percent African American, 11 percent white, and 1 percent Native American. Also, 54 percent of LaGuardia's students are between the ages of 17 and 22, while 14 percent are 30 years or older (www.lagcc.cuny.edu).

Similarly, at Kingsborough College, also in New York City, 42 percent of the students attend part-time, 40 percent have an annual income of less than $20,000, and 48 percent are from the United States. In 2008–2009, more than 70 different languages were spoken by students at Kingsborough (www.kbcc.cuny.edu/). In contrast to these two colleges, of the 12,000 students at Delta College in Michigan, nearly 81 percent are white and less than 1 percent are international. Among these students in 2010, 62 percent are 24 years old or younger, and 57 percent attend part-time (www.delta.edu/aboutdelta).

To continue to show the range of diversity at U.S. community colleges: at Cerritos College in California in 2010, 54 percent of the students are Hispanic, 13 percent are Asian, and 13 percent are white (http://cms.cerritos.edu). At Miami Dade College in Florida in 2010, 78 percent of the students are Hispanic, 61 percent attend part-time, 58 percent are female, and the average age is 26 (www.mdc.edu). Collin College in Texas has a similar percentage of part-time students—62 percent; however, of the 51,000 students enrolled at the college, 61 percent are white, 11 percent are Hispanic, and 11 percent are African American. Among these students in 2010, 9 percent are between the ages of 13 and 17, 48 percent are between the ages of 18 and 22, and 16 percent are 36 years or older (www.collin.edu).

In addition to the diversity of students, community colleges— and even individual campuses of any one college—vary considerably. At Maricopa Community College in Arizona, more than 260,000 students are enrolled at ten different colleges around Phoenix, several of which have more than one campus (www.maricopa. edu). At Tampa, Florida's Hillsborough Community College, which enrolls 48,000 students, campus sizes ranged in 2009–2010 from less than 5,000 at the South Shore campus to more than 22,000 at the Dale Mabry campus (www.hccfl.edu/).

Overall, of the 73,000 students at the six campuses of Northern Virginia Community College (NOVA), 41 percent are 25 years or older, 62 percent attend part-time, and 12 percent are international students. However, at the different campuses, the percentage of male students ranged in 2009–2010 from 22 to 51 percent, the percent of white students ranges from 37 to 58 percent, and the percent of African-American students ranges from 10 to 27 percent (www. nvcc.edu).

Obviously, then, you can see that because community colleges differ in their student populations, they will also differ in their organization and structure. For example, community colleges have both full-time instructors and part-time, adjunct instructors. At some colleges, instructors generally hold office hours, while on other campuses some instructors may even though others do not. Some colleges have orientation while others do not; some have advising offices and/or online advisors; many assign students to developmental courses while others do not; some have health and counseling centers; and some offer community service and study abroad opportunities yet others do not.

We have tried to provide here some evidence of just a few of the ways that community colleges differ, school to school. In this book we have tried to address the specific features, structures, and nomenclature of the community college, generally speaking, but on occasion you may find that a specific example or tip may name a program or regulation differently than what it is called at your college or may discuss a program, requirement, or opportunity in a way that differs from how it is managed on your campus. Again, we suggest you use those occasions to broaden your awareness of community college practice across the country.

Our greatest hope is that the tips in this book help you learn, succeed, graduate, and have a rewarding and fulfilling experience at your community college.

PART 1

THE SUCCESSFUL COLLEGE STUDENT

CHAPTER

1

The Top 10 Tips for College Success and Happiness

1. Believe in Yourself

We can't overstate the importance of maintaining your self-confidence at college. You are bright and capable and—no matter what kind of academic record you had in the past—if you have good study habits and the desire to succeed, you will do just that. Know that this is true, remind yourself daily, and never question your intellectual abilities.

Many students, when they have spoken openly to us, wondered aloud whether they made a mistake in enrolling. This even includes those who may feel overly qualified in class, but who, deep down in a vulnerable place inside them, imagine that they don't really belong in college. After all, they wonder, how can they measure up to all those other smart students now sitting with them in college and actually be capable of doing college level work? This is especially true for students who have not been in a school setting for a while or those who are nervous about being less technologically proficient.

We experienced this same fear when we attended college many years ago. Both of us were good students in high school, but we worried that we would be found out once we got to college. And returning to school after being away for several years only intensified this feeling.

If such a feeling should ever come over you, let go of it immediately. You are capable of doing outstanding work. The key is discovering what your interests are, meeting good students and faculty, and developing good study skills.

When you hear others talk about all the smart people at college, know that they're talking about you. Your high school GPA? Forget it. After the first few weeks of college, high school will seem like years in the past. Your grades from the courses you took six years ago? Forget those too. No one is interested. What faculty members and the other students will be interested in is you today, in your ideas, your interests, what you care about, books you are reading, which classes you are taking, the papers you are writing now, and what you hope to accomplish in your life.

You should approach your college education with full confidence that you will graduate. And your expectation should not be just that you will graduate but that you will excel. In college you will begin the path of realizing your academic, professional, and personal dreams.

If you begin to doubt yourself, try some old fashioned "self talk." Tell yourself: *I know I am smart. I know I can do well in college. I believe in myself and in my academic abilities. I can achieve to the top of my ability. I can accomplish great things.* If it helps, write this somewhere, and put it in an accessible place so that you can read it to yourself as often as you need. Self-confidence is your first insurance policy for success in college.

2. Learn to Be a College Student

Community college is an entirely different universe than high school, the military, or any previous jobs you have held. Your task now is to explore that new universe as you move on to the rest of your life. Community college is a far richer, more substantive, and deeper learning environment than high school. It's important to come to college mentally prepared and with the right expectations for your college experience. Get ready to immerse yourself in an entirely different type and quality of learning.

Whether you graduated recently or years ago, never graduated, or are still in high school, the worst mistake you can make is to imagine that community college is like high school. That's a nightmarish vision. Whether you enjoyed high school or have unhappy memories of it, you don't want to waste these next several years of your life repeating the past.

By the end of twelve years of primary and secondary school, Americans have typically been introduced to five areas of intellectual thought—math, science, English, U.S. history, and often a second language. These are certainly important fields, and they are included among the subjects taught in community college. But the *way* that these and other subjects are taught in college is very different. You should understand that the focus in college is on ideas and on concepts and on using them to understand and solve problems in your life and in the world.

In the effort to help guide you in the process of broadening your intellectual horizons, colleges require you to select courses from a variety of disciplinary and general studies areas. Unfortunately, some students—often ones who feel that they must hurry to achieve their career goals—try to avoid requirements completely, skipping over the general education and recommended preparatory courses. Others approach these requirements as unpleasant chores that they need to get out of the way. And, of course, many students simply don't know how to approach selecting courses and making an educational plan. We urge you to recognize that exciting learning opportunities are ahead of you, especially if you develop a balanced approach to selecting your courses.

What steps can you take in your first year to embrace the best that your community college has to offer?

1. Take a small class that emphasizes discussion. You will get to know your instructor and peers as you explore the subject matter and readings. See also Tip 7 in Chapter 5.

2. Take courses with good teachers. Regardless of how interested you are in any given course content or course description, you are better off selecting your courses on the basis of the best teachers you can find. See also Tip 2 in Chapter 5.

3. Try out a new idea. Considering different ways of thinking about an issue is the very essence of college. College is a place filled with people—including you—who explore and challenge ideas. This is a chance you must not miss out on, a chance to test out your ideas. See also Tip 1 in Chapter 5.

4. Try out a new field of study that you've never considered before. Take a course in some field in which you know very little or even nothing. Take some intellectual risks, please! See also Tip 4 in Chapter 5.

5. Imagine a new career. Try out what life might be like for you if you chose to be an artist, a teacher, a small business owner, a welder, a nurse, an interpreter, a lawyer, a community organizer, or a forest ranger. See also Tip 1 in Chapter 5 and Tip 2 in Chapter 7.

6. Make new friends. Students in your college will be of all different ages and come from all backgrounds and lifestyles, and you should meet new people and learn about their experiences, ideas, and perspectives on the world. See also Tip 5 in Chapter 5.

7. Try out a new perspective. See the world from a point of view of someone who has different interests, comes from a different part of the country, or is of a different gender or race. See also Tip 7 in Chapter 6.

3. Get to Know Your Instructors

Getting to know instructors must be one of your top priorities. It will make your community college experience better. Don't consider yourself a successful student if you don't know at least one college instructor well enough to ask a question, ask for advice, discuss some academic topic, and request a letter of recommendation for jobs, scholarships, awards, internships, and further education. Until you do this, you haven't completed your college education. And if you know one or more instructors well and you're not an A or B student, you have greatly increased the chances that you will walk at graduation alongside your peers. Our experience is that most students who succeed in college have good relationships with one or more instructors.

How should you think about your instructors? Don't be intimidated! Try imagining him or her as a parent, a child, a sibling. An instructor is someone who is like you, but who also likes to spend much of his or her day reading, creating, thinking, discovering, experimenting, writing, and engaging in interesting discussions with people just like you.

Getting to know your instructors is a unique opportunity. You get to spend two or more years in their classes, their studios, and their offices, during which time your primary purpose is to pursue ideas and the intellectual life. It's in this sense that college is so different from other environments. Community college instructors are deeply committed to quality teaching, and they are also passionate about their fields of study. They are delighted to connect with you and to have you join them in their journey during your short stay in their environment. Don't miss out!

The best way to meet instructors is by taking a small discussion class so that personal relationships naturally develop. You see the instructor a few times a week in class; he or she debates ideas with you, reads your papers, and observes your work in class, providing you with insightful feedback. As a result, you'll likely feel comfortable meeting with them after class or during office hours.

There are a couple approaches you can use to get to know your instructors. You can, of course, email or go up to your instructor after class to follow up on a question that was raised in class. Another is to seek out classes or work opportunities that provide closer contact with instructors. This might be a small discussion class, a workshop, or a work study position. These opportunities, and others like them, are described in Tip 7 in Chapter 5.

A second effective approach is to meet with your professor during his or her office hours. In fact, this is one of the most important steps you can take as a student. Tip 3 in Chapter 3 explains in greater detail how you can take advantage of office hours to help you succeed in courses and develop a good working relationship with your instructors.

When it comes time to decide who you should ask to write letters of recommendation, you will be glad you have taken the time to build good relationships with your instructors. In most cases, you will be rewarded with such kind words in the letter that you'll find yourself thrilled at how proud the academic world is of your intellectual pursuits and accomplishments.

4. Get Involved and Be Engaged

It is important to your success in college that you feel an attachment to the institution and are involved in campus life. Not only is this important for your mental and emotional well-being, but it is also a central ingredient for your academic success. In our experience, students who feel connected to their community college are much more likely to do well there, go on to graduate, and report having had positive college experiences.

It's probably easier at first glance to understand the importance of being involved if you are attending a large community college. If you have just come from a high school or workplace or perhaps a neighborhood in which it seemed just about everyone knew, admired, and cared about you, you may naturally feel isolated and lonely. How will you ever stand out and be noticed?

If you are attending a smaller community college, you may anticipate that you've already addressed this concern. But in a surprising way, the experience of a small college can result in some feelings that are very similar to those of your peers at larger ones. And if you find yourself feeling isolated or lonely at a smaller school, it's likely that you'll attribute these feelings to something in you rather than to the college's size or impersonal atmosphere. It's possible that at a community college where everyone appears to be nice and interested in each individual and where students know one another, you can still feel like an outsider on the periphery.

What do you do? The simple answer is to get involved. And to get involved, you may want to attempt a variety of strategies. You can take advantage of academic structures whose very purpose is to create more personal learning environments. Some of these—like small discussion classes, learning communities, and community service learning—are described in Chapters 5 and 6. You can also get involved in campus activities, events, and organizations. Every college has a myriad of student organizations to suit your interests in politics, sports, media, art, music and theater, writing, race and ethnicity, religion, and so on. For more, see Tip 10 in Chapter 5.

The opportunities are there. Try one. In fact, try more than one, and try reaching beyond just those that have worked for you in the past.

5. Expand Your Comfort Zone ⟶

The first days of college can be rather intimidating socially. After four or more years in high school with the same group of friends or years working, serving in the military, or raising children, you may have already established a reputation among your peers and teachers or in your community as a leader and a very special person. Yet you now have to start all over. Or so it seems at the time. At this anxious moment, many students are inclined to withdraw to what feels most comfortable and familiar.

The friends you already have are important, but it's a mistake to retreat to them just for security. Many community college students come from neighborhoods and schools that are highly segregated by race, religion, and class. If you retreat to the comfort zone of your past, it's as if you are locking yourself in your room and imposing a strict curfew on yourself.

In college you have the opportunity to meet and learn with a whole range of new people with different backgrounds and different ideas from yours. They may see the world through very different lenses. Getting to know the world through their lenses in addition to your own will sharpen your vision, expand your ability to understand other perspectives, and deepen your learning and cognitive understanding of coursework.

If you have never traveled far from your home community or if you are a recent immigrant or international student, introduce yourself to other new students. In what ways do they view politics and interpret books differently or the same as you do? If you come from a liberal background, talk to a conservative student and find out that person's perspective. If you are young, work in a group with students who are older and who maybe have children your age. What do you have in common, and in what ways are your worlds so different that it takes a special effort to speak a common language?

The people that you meet in your classes are important resources, and you should take advantage of opportunities to study in groups, work on homework, and form friendships with those who are very different from you. Students in diverse classrooms often learn more deeply and understand issues in a more complex fashion. Developing the ability to study with others also translates to the workplace. Students who embrace the diversity of their post high school settings are better prepared for participating in a diverse workforce and supervising or being supervised by a wide range of people. Appreciating diversity provides the opportunity for America to realize its highest democratic ideals.

Perhaps most important for you as an individual, if you choose to take advantage of the diverse student body of your campus, you are likely to have a much richer and expansive life. Your opportunity for friendship and broad thinking will have fewer restrictions or boundaries.

6. Learn to Study Effectively

It may come as a surprise that, for many students, college success is as much a result of good study skills as it is of intellectual ability or "smarts." That's right. One of the most important keys to academic success in college is having good study skills. You have already completed high school or your GED, so you have learned how to succeed. But translating your intellectual abilities into passing grades in college requires a fair amount of new expertise in the how-to of studying and reading and writing for college.

This is so important that we have provided extensive details about it in the next three parts of this book. For now, however, we would like to emphasize that you should develop a study routine that works for you as an individual. As we explain in the following parts, you will want to decide where and what time of day to study and determine the conditions that work best for you for each of your courses and maybe even for different kinds of assignments. You may find that you can concentrate at home for some assignments but need a library or empty classroom for reading difficult material.

Some students—even those who have been used to receiving good grades—aren't prepared for all the reading required in college courses. However, reading is one of the most important skills for college success. By this, we mean a whole range of reading skills. You will want to become an active or critical reader. You will need to learn how to approach your reading before you ever read a word and how to test your comprehension while you read and once you finish. To do this, you will need to learn effective techniques for annotating—that is, for making effective notes in the margins of your book while you read. (This means, of course, that you will need to buy and use the books required for your classes!)

It is also essential that you learn to read the wide range of text assignments in different ways. Reading history or chemistry textbooks requires a different approach than reading fiction. Scholarly journal articles and academic monographs require yet another level of focus and concentration to fully comprehend the research findings, empirical analysis, and theoretical discussion they reflect.

Your reading skills will also help you in other ways. As you begin a specific assignment, go back and carefully reread the assignment. Make sure you have understood all the important elements. It is absolutely frustrating to work for hours on something only to realize that you didn't fully and precisely address the assignment. Be certain you understand what is expected, and don't hesitate to contact the instructor for clarification if you have any questions. This helpful step is possible, of course, only if you haven't delayed doing the assignment until right before it is due.

Finally, you will want to learn how to write for college courses. There are always some students who believe that, while they must keep up with their daily assignments, they can easily put off essays and research papers until a few days or even the night before the due date. Putting off the work of some classes is a certain path to eventual trouble. Writing papers requires a process of thinking, rethinking, drafting, revising, rethinking again, redrafting again, and so on. Every paper you turn in should represent your very best work. It should be, at the very least, your third carefully revised draft. And reaching the third draft should represent a process of thinking, composing, and rethinking of the content, language, style, and of course technical aspects of the paper.

Because community colleges recognize how important study skills and college-level reading and writing are, they administer English and math placement tests to entering students. These tests signal courses that students may be required to take. Policies differ from college to college. At some colleges, you might be required to enroll immediately in specific classes in English, math, or reading, or even a combination of those. At some colleges, students are required to take reading and/or college skills classes, but at others, they are not. Some colleges will require developmental math or English prior to enrolling in college-level math or English but permit students to enroll in other college-level classes. However, these skills are so important to your success in all subjects that we urge you not to delay taking these skill-development classes. Many colleges also offer reading and study skills classes. Even the brightest and best-prepared students gain valuable new skills in these classes. Consider taking one or more. The time invested in developing these skills early in your college career will save you much valuable time (and anxiety) later.

Whatever you do, don't sell yourself short in these areas. Do a good, honest assessment of how you study, read, and write, and make adjustments and improvements as needed. If you find yourself in need of help in this area, don't hesitate to ask for advice and suggestions very early in your community college career.

7. Know Where to Find Help and Ask for It

Some students think that asking for academic help is just for those who are considered "at risk." In college, the whole notion of asking for academic help is entirely different. Being able to ask for help is crucial, and the first step is admitting to yourself that you should want and need help. Higher education is about scholarly inquiry, and colleges are comprised of people who are genuinely interested in discovering, studying, learning, analyzing, creating, and sharing new knowledge. In that context, everyone in college, including instructors, is in constant search of deeper, clearer understandings and new insights. If you don't understand the complexities of an argument, you are expected to ask. If you miss the meaning of a lecture, you should ask about it. If the math assignments or readings are not clear, without question, you should ask for clarification.

Knowing where to find help and being willing to use that help are so important that we have devoted an entire part of this book to it (Part 3). For starters, however, we suggest that you familiarize yourself with some of the key resources for academic support.

First, learn how your college organizes academic advising. Your first stop for academic assistance, and it should be a frequent stop, should be with an academic advisor. A good advisor can help you save time and money and avoid unnecessary frustrations. Advisors know the academic rules for course and graduation requirements. They are familiar with course offerings and sequences at your college. They are also often familiar with the transfer requirements for four-year colleges in your area or with employment opportunities for professional-technical programs. If they don't know, they can help you figure out how to find what these are. Advisors will try to help you make decisions about your community college plans rather than outline plans for you. After all, this is your education, not theirs. It is crucial that you figure out what holds most meaning for your studies, your career, and your life.

Second, learn as much as you can about the support services available to students at your college. Find out what kinds of support centers, computer labs, and learning labs are available on your campus. Most have writing centers and/or tutoring services, and most have courses specifically designed for international students. Some colleges offer orientations to college resources and/or college skills. Some offer courses that teach successful note-taking strategies, how to organize effective study groups, or how to do better on tests. Many colleges offer workshops, not just for beginning students but those who are ready to transfer and/or look for work.

You should also know that community college libraries are much more comprehensive, sophisticated, and technologically advanced than most neighborhood libraries. Community college librarians help students learn to access computer databases and find appropriate college-level sources in print and online for research papers. They also offer more basic assistance, such as giving tours of the library and helping find books. Most college librarians are on the cutting edge of technological advances and can be of great assistance in helping you get your hands and eyes on the astounding resources available to students and scholars today.

Remember, if you're not asking for help and taking advantage of advising, study groups, tutors, and academic support services, you're not being a smart student. Most of your learning will take place outside of the classroom, and you must be skilled and assertive to be sure your academic learning both inside and outside of class is as high quality and intensive as it can be.

8. Discover the Value of Challenging Ideas (Including Your Own)

The first day of college represents a momentous change in your life. Perhaps you are just months out of high school or have decided to return after several years to complete your community college degree. Or perhaps you have left your full-time job to prepare for a new career. The change to community college studies is particularly dramatic for young students, but it can be very unsettling for older students as well. This is the time to begin taking responsibility to think and express your own ideas, thoughts, and opinions.

Whatever your age, you might want to examine the extent to which your family, teachers, peers, and social institutions have taught you to think and act in particular ways. You may have been taught how to interpret history, told what books to read, or may have been directed—explicitly or through subtle pressure—toward certain groups of people. College students are expected to begin to assert themselves as independent thinkers and to voice their own ideas, interpretations, and analyses. They must learn to explain their ideas, opinions, values, decisions, and actions and to provide reliable and credible evidence to support those. This is difficult, but embrace this opportunity! Don't shy away from it.

Think carefully about all that you are exposed to. Start asking why you believe the things you believe. Whether you reaffirm or modify your beliefs or adopt new ones, what's important is that you take responsibility and ownership of your life and your society and the journey that is yours.

In the classroom as in life, ask hard questions. Challenge your instructors about what they tell you as fact or what they offer as interpretation. How did they come to that opinion? Look for the evidence and the research behind their analyses. Do the careful reading that is essential to asking good questions. Challenge the authors that you read. Become a critical and serious thinker. See also Tip 5 in Chapter 5. Be thoughtful in your self-reflection, and be critical in questioning the ideas, assertions, and analyses of others.

9. Make Friends with Staff in the Financial Aid Office

A college education is going to cost a substantial amount of money. For most, it's money you don't have. Hopefully, you've already made the correct and necessary decision that you should not forgo a community college education because of the price tag. However, to find a way to pay for college—whether through grants, loans, work-study, or a combination of all three—you will eventually end up dealing with your financial aid office.

Welcome to the world of bureaucracy! Beginning with the infamous FAFSA form (or whatever may replace it in the future as the financial aid process continually changes), you will be working with layers of organizations that provide financial aid funds. Your main contact will be your financial aid office, but along the way you will learn that the U.S. government and its various agencies, banks, and loan institutions, and sometimes the state government and various other offices as well, are all part of the picture.

You and/or your family will need to be very organized about financial aid. It's a bad joke, but you almost need a college degree to fill out these forms. It certainly may feel that way when you face all those questions for the very first time. Get all your tax documents together way ahead of time, and buy some file folders to keep all the records and correspondence that will take place in the years ahead.

Make a point of getting to know a counselor at the financial aid office. Make these people your friends, not your enemies. They can help you make sense of the myriad rules and regulations—and they change every year—and to try to assign the proper amount of aid to each applicant. They want to award you aid if you qualify. They will answer your questions about the process for applying, timelines, and forms. Treat them as people, not bureaucrats, and you will have much greater success and much less frustration in your efforts.

If ever there was a time and a place to ask questions, the financial aid process and office is it. When you first start working on the financial aid forms, come to the office with your questions. If you get a financial aid notification letter that is unclear, call the office and ask them to explain.

If you disagree with the financial aid office's assessment of your earnings or if you are concerned that the award you have received isn't sufficient, call the office. You'll probably be frustrated or discouraged (especially if you're put on hold), but don't shout at them. In almost all cases, they will be happy to review your file with you and offer various alternatives for you to think about in terms of financial aid.

During the academic year or when tuition bills arrive, if the award doesn't show up or if you haven't received the amount you expected, don't panic. Just arrange a time that you can meet with someone in the financial aid office to look at your file. Depending on the time of the term, you might have to wait, so make sure to schedule enough time to be able to meet with the staff. Bring your own well-organized financial aid file with you to help make your case. In the event you need an emergency loan or if you've over-spent part of your budget that should have gone toward financial aid, talk with someone in this office for advice on how to proceed. Staff in the office will also likely know whether the college has special programs that allow students to pay tuition in installments or ones that provide funds for buying books or help dealing with short-term financial emergencies.

Colleges want you to have enough funds to pay tuition. Think of them as your allies in the financial aid game. Most likely you won't get as much aid as you want or need, but the financial aid counselors want to be sure you are treated as fairly as the regulations will allow. They also want you to graduate and have a rewarding experience.

This is a very important relationship for you. Make it a good one.

10. Stay Positive and Learn to Be Comfortable with Transitions and Change

The adrenaline rush in the first term of college can seem over-whelming. The highs and lows of classes and the shifts in social relationships can be as exciting as they can seem devastating. It's about making a major change in your life. It's about all the new people you are meeting and all the new ideas you are confronting. Some are glorious and provoke highs you may not have felt before; others are sad, depressing, and painful.

Know that you'll always get through the tough moments. Some of these are predictable: getting lost on the first day, taking the first exam, writing the first paper, discovering you are the oldest person in the class. Some days will be neverending, and then there will be a transportation breakdown, a critical comment from an instructor, a bad phone call from a family member, a rejection, or a conflict with the college bureaucracy. How could it get so bad, you will wonder. And, then, just as suddenly, there will be a phone call from a classmate to find out how you are doing, an A on a quiz, a quiet walk across campus, or admission into your program.

Remember that major transitions in our lives are accompanied by moments that can be both exhilarating and chaotic. Trust your own inner strength and flexibility to help keep you buoyant. Take life one day at a time, and cherish each moment (except the forgettable ones—learn from those moments and then forget them forever). Store the best experiences in your permanent memory bank. Make a list of your best ideas for tomorrow and for the long term. Remind yourself that you'll quickly get past the trying moments. Make the good days last a lifetime.

PART 2

THE FUNDAMENTALS OF COLLEGE SUCCESS

CHAPTER

2

Classroom Fundamentals: Learn the Basics of Being a College Student

1. Think of Yourself as a Learner

Some students worry that they are not good students. They express deep concerns about having been out of school for a long time, about previously not having done well in their classes, or that they are not fluent in academic English. Fortunately, your English language skills, the kind of student you were in the past, and whether or not you are required to take developmental classes matters far less than the fact that you are now not just a student, but also a learner. College teaches you to learn in ways that will help you in all facets of your life. Everything that you have learned in your life has come from building on what you know and practice. Your willingness to work hard has helped you take the small, consistent incremental steps needed to develop the expertise you already have. The same principle works in college as you learn and develop new expertise to help you succeed in all facets of your life.

Aren't all students learners? Not necessarily. Some students, even sometimes those who have always received good grades, just go through the motions. They do what it takes to receive their grades. They prepare for and pass tests, but they are not working to their full potential. Too often, they focus on grades rather than on learning and, as a result, discover that they recall little of value from the courses they have taken.

Learners recognize that learning is a process. Any successes you've had are not the result of luck, and are not due to an instructor's attitude toward you. Learners recognize the importance of mistakes and failures. All good learners—whether athletes, doctors, or welders—are willing to analyze mistakes and to learn from them. An example of this is the student who feels that he or she hasn't been able to write but who is willing to learn from mistakes and finds that writing better papers is easier. A student who always found it easy to write may find the opposite in college. This is why students who have been away from school for a while tend to do well when they return to school; they are now prepared to apply what they have learned outside of school about how to succeed.

Many successful coaches insist that players should never look at the scores that are already on the scoreboard and that they should pay no attention to what other teams (students) are doing. Instead, players should concentrate on doing their absolute best, learning from every moment of play, and focusing on what they can control—their own efforts. These coaches believe that if the players do that, the scoreboard will take care of itself.

This is good advice for students also. If you focus on your learning, if you practice, if you reflect on what is and is not working, and if you analyze how you can do better, you will find that it doesn't matter what kind of student you were in the past or whether you are fluent in academic English. You will learn. And the "scoreboard" will take care of itself.

2. Balance the Many Demands on Your Time

Community college students pursue their studies with a remarkable array of responsibilities, perhaps more than any other type of students in the country. Some of you are still in high school and may not be attending college full-time. Some of you have graduated in the past couple of years, and some have been out of school for decades. You are likely to be financially responsible for yourself and to work full- or part-time. Many of you care for children at home as a single parent or as part of a couple. Some of you may have attended schools that did not prepare you well for college right after high school. Some of you have come to the United States from other countries and are still mastering English. Also, some of you are the first in your families to attend college, so you may not have access to all of the resources that help people in college.

How is it, then, that so many of you overcome such great odds to become successful? The real secret to success in community college is to understand how to prioritize among competing demands. Take small, incremental steps to build your expertise. Accept that taking risks and failing are a necessary part of the process. Success requires faith and trust in yourself.

As a community college student, you will likely find yourself handling a lot of demands on your time. You might be trying to coordinate a rigorous schedule of courses, or your work and school schedules, or the schedules at your college and your children's schools. You might be trying to balance the demands of a research class with long hours of preparation for a work presentation. You might be weighing your academic pressures with the needs of your family.

Instead of being alarmed or frustrated by all this, you can recognize that, having taken the risk to enroll in college, you are already engaged in the process of being a college student. Now you just need to remind yourself to trust the process, to take it one step at a time, to practice, and to learn what does and doesn't work for you. Remind yourself that you need both intense focus and the ability to relax. Remind yourself that you may need to focus first on one task, then two, and then three. If at times you feel you have too many "balls in the air," remember that you can always step back and reprioritize. Review what you already know about how to succeed and, most important, trust yourself and focus on the toss.

3. Ask Questions

Since the first grade, teachers have been telling you that there is no such thing as a bad question, but you believe that they didn't mean it because you saw a student in class get ridiculed for asking just that—a "bad" question.

We can't promise you that you won't be ridiculed by instructors, family, and friends for asking questions, but we can tell you that if you don't ask questions, and as often as necessary, you might as well not be in college. For students who are new to the United States, know that asking questions is culturally acceptable and expected.

Questioning is at the core of intellectual life. It comes from basic human curiosity. Its source is our need to explore what isn't yet understood, discover the unknown, examine the truths behind the truth, and develop the capacity to see from multiple perspectives. Questioning allows our social and scientific worlds to advance from one generation to the next.

Asking questions is also a very practical matter. You need to know where your class is going to be held so you can be there on time on the first day of class. You need to know whether classes start on the hour, on the half hour, or at ten minutes past the hour. You need to know whether to address your instructors by their titles or by their first names. You need to know when your first exam is due and what your instructor thinks about using websites as sources for research papers. You will need to learn the hours for the computer lab and all the different options for tutoring help. You most certainly will need to ask how to access the rich virtual and print resources of your library. Although it is often possible to find answers to these questions on the college website or course syllabus, if you can't find the information or are unsure about it, by all means ask the question.

Similarly, in your personal life, you might need to learn how to reprioritize the demands in your life to handle school as well as your family and job. You will need to know what to do when your hard drive crashes just as you were finishing an important assignment. You may even need to learn how to do laundry or open a bank account and balance a checkbook.

Questioning is also political. Asking questions is a statement that you have the right and the responsibility to question authorities and to question authority itself. You have the right to schedule an appointment with your instructor to ask why he or she does not hold office hours or frequently misses classes. If you try this and are unable to resolve a serious issue about your grade, you have the right to meet with other administrators. You have the responsibility to ask the president of your college why there is such a high ratio of part-time to full-time instructors. You have the right to challenge the news media's depiction of current events. You have the responsibility to ask students in your course chat rooms or at your lunch table why they are laughing at racist jokes. You have the responsibility to ask why more students are not voting in campus elections for student leaders or in national presidential and congressional elections.

It's true that some questions will irritate and agitate others and may complicate your life. However, that doesn't mean that the questions are "bad." Be respectful, but keep asking your questions—that's the role of an active and successful learner.

4. Return to the Three Rs—Reading, 'Riting, and 'Rithmetic

Now that you've entered college, you may be feeling both very confident in your academic abilities and at the same time embarrassed that you still need help with some of the basic foundational learning skills. Far too many students, both those from weak high schools as well as those from high schools considered in the top 10 in the country, still need some instruction and support in one or more areas of the "basics." Be sure to get this additional instruction and support whether or not you are assigned to developmental classes. If you have tested below college level in any skill area, make sure you enroll immediately in the courses that will prepare you for success.

Even more distressing than the fact that too many students have inadequate skills in the basics is that there is shame associated with it. Students far too often will try to hide their lack of skills in these areas, and instructors far too often do not challenge students to get the instructional support they need.

You can learn all of these skills. And, because you are in community college, almost all of which have numerous kinds of academic resource centers and support services, you have a unique opportunity to learn these skills. Don't try to use your smarts to hide gaps in your previous training: Get assistance! After you graduate from college, you might not have the chance or desire to go back to revisit those areas in which you are weak academically. If you feel bad enough now to hide these skill problems, you will feel much worse later. Now is the time!

Why didn't you learn all the necessary skills in high school? In some cases, even though you are a bright person and a good student, your K–12 schools may not have provided the foundational needs that you required in a whole range of areas. In other cases, educational policy in some well-intentioned schools has tipped too far toward an emphasis on broader themes of learning, with the result that basic skills did not receive sufficient emphasis.

If you find yourself in this situation, drop any low self-image or feeling of embarrassment at needing help. This is not a test of your intellectual ability—these are important skills. Give yourself an emotional break with this.

Go to your community college's website or talk to your advisor, your instructor, or your friends to find out where the academic resource center is located. Set up a first appointment, and plan on coming back for an entire term. More than likely it will take some time to fully learn these skills. Finally, go on with your life and enjoy! Know that your decision to get help means you're going to do great work in college and beyond.

5. Go to Class

Yes, it's important to go to class! You should plan to attend every class session. You have decided to attend college, and it is the opportunity of a lifetime. Of course, in real life emergencies do occur that might cause you to miss a class, so be sure to learn the attendance policy for each class. Take advantage of every chance you have to learn.

Most students do attend class regularly, but we are often surprised by some of the explanations for missing class. Some students have trouble waking up in time for early morning classes or they equate being in college with "being able to skip class." Others have enrolled in classes that conflict with their sports teams' schedule or their choir or play rehearsals. Some have scheduled an appointment with an advisor or tutor for the same time. While these activities are important, they should not ever take priority over your academic work.

Students enrolled in online classes sometimes give priority to their traditional classes or put off checking in until they have days off work. If you are enrolled in an online course or in a "hybrid" course (one that meets both in a classroom and online), you should plan to check in as many times a week as a traditional class would meet—for instance, at least three times a week for a three-credit course or five times a week for a five-credit course.

You need to think carefully about how you approach being a college student. To be worthwhile, college has to be both a choice and a priority for you. If you don't want to be in college or if it is not a priority for you, then by all means save yourself a lot of money and time and take a leave of absence. However, as long as you are in college, remember that each course you take holds immense possibilities; each course period has been carefully planned and is important. You should want to be there for each session.

There is another reason to attend regularly. Despite your best efforts, at times events happen that are outside your control, like an injury, a family member's illness, or a sudden loss of transportation to college. Some students find that their family and work responsibilities begin to conflict with their course schedules. The term breaks for K–12 schools and community colleges seldom match, and even students who have carefully arranged their work schedules may suddenly be required to attend a staff training retreat or cover a shift for a co-worker. We have had students who were deployed by the military during midterms or who went into labor and gave birth to a child right before a final exam. It will be far easier to negotiate options with your instructors when these types of things happen if you have been attending regularly and your coursework is up to date.

Embrace the opportunity you have to attend community college. Be sure to take advantage of every opportunity available to you. But keep your eye on the academic prize, even while you are involved in the whole community college learning experience. The first step is to attend classes.

6. Arrive on Time, Turn Off Your Cell Phone, and Follow the Rules of the Classroom

One of the delights of the community college classroom, compared to K–12 classes, is that there are relatively few discipline problems. Students know they are in college to learn, whether they are in classes to fulfill requirements for a four-year college or are in ESL, developmental, or workforce training classes. They are there by choice, not by parental or state law and, for the most part, they act like adult learners. This means that there is an expectation that you will behave in a respectful manner to your instructors and peers and that they will be respectful toward you.

The first sign of respect is to go to class and to go on time. Particularly in a small discussion class, you are responsible for contributing to the course's success. You cannot contribute if you do not attend. Whether you are in a small or large class, when you come to class late, you disrupt and interrupt the lecture or discussion that is in progress.

Turn off your cell phone. Don't send text messages. Don't play games on your phone. All of these behaviors are rude to everyone around you. You have probably heard about the risks of driving while you are talking on the phone or text messaging. You should know that doing so in the college classroom also poses a high risk—a risk to academic success and your relationship with your instructor and your fellow students.

Only open your laptop in class if your instructor allows it. If your instructor encourages you to take notes or to do work on your laptop during class, be sure to stick to the assignment. Don't play computer games or do your social networking while pretending to take notes. Would you like it if you were speaking up during class and your instructor was not paying attention to you because he or she was reading email messages? You might wonder if students use the computer in class only as a result of a boring instructor, but we have seen students reading newspapers, sending texts, and doing crossword puzzles during other students' presentations. We have also listened to many complaints from other students who find it disrespectful and disruptive. It's not acceptable to jeopardize the learning environment for others!

Don't sleep during class. If you are so tired that you can't stay awake, then you shouldn't be in class. No one wants to watch you sleep. Go home, and go to bed.

Don't whisper to your neighbor in class. We see this behavior mostly from students who went to high school together. That they continue to behave like they are in high school is clear to everyone in the class. If you have something so urgent to tell your friend that you must do so during class, then you should leave the classroom, have the conversation elsewhere, and act on the emergency you are facing. Otherwise, don't whisper.

It is a privilege to attend college. We find that first-generation and returning college students are among the most respectful students in class. They seem to have a special appreciation for the power and privilege that are captured in the opportunity to be part of a scholarly community at an institution of higher learning. They are joined by 98–99 percent of their classmates in that respectful behavior. Be a member of this respectful majority, and never forget how fortunate you are.

7. Read the Assignments—All of Them!

No matter how long it has been since you were in high school, you may be surprised to discover that the expectations about reading represent one of the major differences between high school and community college.

A major difference is the amount of reading. Many students are surprised by how much reading is assigned in college—books, academic articles, handouts, and even the syllabus, which instructors expect students to read carefully and keep for future reference.

Another difference is the role of readings in community college courses. In high school, students are tested on just about anything and everything they are assigned to read. In college, regardless of the type of class, the expectation is that you will want to read everything assigned because you want to learn as much as possible and also so that you are prepared for the lectures and other course assignments that are dependent on the readings. If you are tested, it will be in much more comprehensive and analytic ways.

Instructors read everything they can get their hands on. They are constantly trying to get access to the latest works in their field and beyond. When you enter their classes, especially in introductory classes, they assume—usually accurately—that you are interested in the topic but know very little about the subject they are teaching. They feel compelled to load up the readings so that you can enter into the discussion of the topic. In their minds, some foundational theories, arguments, and texts are essential background information to begin the first class discussions.

You, as a typical student, are wondering if all this reading is going to be tested or if you will need to present it all back in a paper. You are thinking, based on your previous experiences, that if the homework is not going to be tested or graded—and certainly if it's not going to be discussed—then there's no need for it to be assigned or for you to read it. Instructors, however, have no interest in listening to you merely repeat back the main points of introductory material. They want to move forward quickly to the much more nuanced literature to begin discussions in class of the more complex issues in the field. They are expecting that you will likely make notes in the margins of your books to pose questions and to make connections to other readings as well as to your personal experiences.

In those subjects in which everyone has personal experience, such as family, gender relations, education, and so on, new students sometimes complain that the readings are just repeating the same obvious point over and over again. If you find yourself making that complaint, step back for a moment and think about how carefully you are reading the assignments. After all, your instructors have spent their entire academic lives reading and researching the topic you are now studying. They are asking you to join them as junior colleagues, going beyond the typical surface-level understandings of the topic to deeper and more complex layers of analysis.

As a college-educated person, you want to understand issues beyond the sound bites you hear on TV news shows or the shouting debates that pit one TV guest versus the next. Those shows give off lots of heat but shed no light and offer no insight. In contrast, in college, the assigned readings and accompanying class discussions will take you beyond the superficial conversations to a different level. Trust the value of assignments.

Society needs college-educated thinkers who have the skills and understanding to analyze the most complex and vexing problems facing the world. Approach all readings not as assignments but as opportunities to become an educated citizen, a well-informed and worldly person, and an analytical thinker. If you read and read deeply, you will begin the process of becoming one of these much needed well-educated citizens.

8. Create Study Groups

Our students offer many different reasons why they do not join or create their own study groups: they don't have time, their schedules are too complex, they don't know many people in class, they are too shy, they think it's too complicated for an online course, or they think they are supposed to learn everything on their own without help. None of these are good reasons to miss out on one of the best strategies for learning. Students learn more and more deeply when they study in groups, work on papers and assignments collaboratively, and have a network of peers to talk about course work.

One of the best ways to test your knowledge and comprehension of ideas and information is to try to explain them to someone else, either in writing or out loud. A study group is an ideal way to do this. Studying regularly with others provides you with quick checks on the accuracy of homework assignments or your understanding of a concept. Students in math classes who are required to check their homework answers with at least one other person find that they learn far more quickly. When they have different answers on a math problem, they can work together to figure out why that happened and which answers are correct. If they can't solve the problem, then they know exactly what they need to ask the instructor to review for the next class session.

When you share notes and review readings with others in a study group, you increase your chances of making sure that you have covered all of the material. You also have a chance to see whether you all agree on which ideas are most important or relevant. If you have not completely understood a reading or a part of a lecture, you have the chance to hear different perspectives on it from other students.

Perhaps the best aspect of a good study group is that studying with others who are committed to their learning can be, and should be, fun. This is not to say that a study session should be entirely social. In fact, it's usually a bad idea to form study groups only with close friends because it is harder to stay focused on the purpose of the group, which is to study and learn. But around exam time or the end of term, after studying together, wrestling with confusing or complex issues, debating answers, and sharing the results of their hard work, study groups generally turn into support groups, with members helping each other deal with stress.

Meet in a place that is both convenient and not distracting. A neutral meeting place is best, like a library conference room or a very quiet coffee shop. Ask your instructor to set up a chat room and discussion board for your group. Or, post a request online to find others who live near you. Meet regularly since a series of shorter sessions will be generally more effective for your learning than one long cram session before a paper or test.

Finally, establish the ground rules that help you stay on task and include everyone's work and ideas. Embrace diversity of the members of the study group, value each person's contribution, and be sure to avoid the trap of falling into old and hurtful stereotypes about which students are most skilled and knowledgeable in different subject areas.

Socializing is important, but you will be more likely to learn, succeed, and enjoy your study group if you make sure that you use your time well and everyone feels respected and comfortable participating to their fullest capability.

9. Be Intellectually Honest: Don't Cheat

In college, academic integrity is an important element. It is the academic equivalent of civil law. Academic integrity is essential to the entire enterprise of scholarly inquiry and intellectual exploration.

One area emphasized at colleges today is the problem of plagiarism. Some students, not being fully aware of what constitutes plagiarism, unknowingly cheat when they use outside sources in their papers. The guidelines and rules for how to use research in your papers and presentations is something that you can and must learn right away.

But other students deliberately cheat.

In any college, cheating is like stealing. If you are caught plagiarizing passages, you will be subject to the rules your college has established for dealing with violations of its academic integrity policies. You will face punishment that can range from a stern warning to a failing grade on a test or an entire course, or suspension or expulsion.

The best and only advice about cheating is to never, ever do it. Your purpose in college is to learn, and you will learn nothing from cheating. You are stealing someone else's ideas in order for you to get a better grade.

There are many views as to why a significant amount of cheating occurs on college campuses. Some people suggest that there is so much stress and competition to get top grades that students feel pressured to break the rules in order to fulfill their professional goals. Others believe it reflects the breakdown of basic values in society, a lack of respect for rules, peers, and authority. For others it's a cultural issue—where using someone else's words is done to show respect for that person.

Whatever their reasons, students plagiarize and cheat (and get caught) in any number of ways. They look over a classmate's shoulder during an exam to get an answer. They copy other students' papers. They buy papers on the Internet. They use pieces of other people's works or paraphrase their ideas without giving any citation. They set up computer programs to use other people's work to complete lab assignments and math problems. Instructors and college administrators know all the tricks of the trade and are quite adept at identifying student cheaters.

The question of academic integrity is a matter of personal integrity. The cheating habits you develop or maintain in college are likely to stay with you throughout your business life and personal relations. If you cheat because you feel unbearable stress in community college, rest assured that the pressure will be much more intense and stressful in the work world. Don't get started down this wrongheaded path. Be better than this.

Live your life honestly so you can wake up every morning proud of your life and proud of all your accomplishments. Examine your ethical makeup and your personal integrity. Set yourself on the right course in college, and it will serve you well throughout your entire life.

10. Make Smart Decisions about Online Courses, Personal Technology, and Social Networks

You are living in a time of enormous technological change. Technology is reshaping our intellectual worlds, our social networks, and our global community, and in your college classes you will find yourself right in the middle of this revolution.

If you are considering taking one or more online classes, you will want to make sure this is the right choice for you. As with traditional classes, look for good instructors and, if possible, small class sizes. Most of all, understand that the abilities that are necessary for success in traditional courses are very much the same as those needed for online ones. Many of our students do very well in online classes while others are adamant that they need the structure of classes that meet regularly and provide the opportunity to learn face-to-face with their instructor and other students. Some students do not realize that online courses can take more work and time than traditional classes.

The important criteria for success in online courses are self-discipline, organization, and time management. The responsibility for learning rests almost entirely on the student in online classes. You should plan to log in several times a week and set aside a block of time each day to read and view material, participate in discussions, practice simulations or problem sets, test your understanding of the subject matter, and write papers. Trying to do all of this once a week or every now and then won't work. Without self-discipline, it is too easy to get behind.

It is also important to have very good reading and writing (and typing!) skills. In addition to assigned readings, it will be crucial to read everything—the syllabus, assignment instructions and evaluation criteria, calendars of deadlines, postings, emails, and even the systemwide announcements about scheduled times that the course management system will not be operating.

You will also need good communication skills. This includes knowing the etiquette for emailing others and participating in chat rooms and discussion boards. And it includes taking the steps to build a good working relationship with your instructor. You should consider emailing at least once a week to check on how you are doing in the course. And, remember, the instructor (and other students) may not respond immediately to your inquiries and posts.

It's also important to have the appropriate technology for an online course. Before enrolling, find out what software you will need and read the course syllabus for information about other technology needs. You will need a reliable and fast computer, a reliable and fast Internet connection, a flash drive or other convenient system for backing up your work, and a back-up plan in case you have problems with any of these.

You might discover that you are as current on technology developments as many of the faculty and staff on campus. However, if you are not, you should get up to speed. If you haven't had the same access to technology for educational and networking purposes as your peers, then ask questions, experiment, and accept offers of help from your classmates or from the staff at the library and in computer labs.

As for social networking, embrace it, have fun with it, and use it for its potential for personal, professional, and political opportunities, but understand the possible dangers and downsides of an increasingly open, networked global society. The networked technological world includes people who use technology for their own profit, whatever the cost to others. Whenever you are contemplating sharing personal or financial information about yourself or friends, keep in mind that those people are on the same network sites. So be sure to protect yourself, your personal information, and your privacy.

Finally, as technologically networked at you may be, learn how to be effective personally and educationally in your communication and networks. Avoid interrupting conversations to take a phone call. Don't send text messages while talking with faculty during office hours. Don't go online to social network sites during class. Be as personable, confident, and sensitive when you are in the moment and in the physical space of others as you can be when you are in the virtual world.

3

Resource Fundamentals: Listen to Advice and Be Open to Support

1. Pay Attention at Orientation

A great thing about college is that all students are considered adults. But it's important to remember that this means that all of your decisions about courses matter and that your signature for tuition payments, apartment leases, and various purchases has significant associated costs. If you have not done so already, start reading every item related to your enrollment—each one.

You can start by carefully reading all mail and email. If required, be sure to send in your enrollment deposit, sign up for orientation, complete all your financial aid forms, pick up your student identification card, and purchase your bus or parking pass. Record important deadlines on your calendar, particularly those for fees, registration, and adding and dropping classes. Learn whether your college has a waiting list for classes, and find out the policies about wait lists. If you plan to rent an apartment, look for one now.

Go to orientation, even if it is optional. At orientation, read everything more carefully and take detailed notes, especially about dates, deadlines, and people to contact when you have questions. Read the college catalog (in print or online). To be sure, it's boring. But it also serves as the community college's academic contract with you. It will tell you what core or general education/distribution courses are required for you to graduate.

The college catalog and the course schedules provide you with the academic calendar, so you will know when the term or semester starts, when final exams and term breaks are held, and whether there are days that classes will be cancelled or the college will be closed. Make sure you read these dates carefully before you schedule an extra shift at work or plan a trip. The community college materials will include campus maps, which, as hard as they may be to read, will come in handy on the first day of class when you're lost and need to get to a class in a big hurry. Mark on your map where your classes meet. Carry the map with you.

Read the course guide and time schedule carefully. Read about all the courses that are open to you, which do and do not have prerequisites—required test scores or courses that must be completed first. Find out how many credits are needed for full-time enrollment or to qualify for financial aid. Check when and how often courses meet. Note additional hours for lab or studio sessions. Look carefully to see when ESL or developmental courses are required or when four-year transfer college courses are required. Plan your schedule around these courses. Check out the rules about dropping and adding classes with or without penalties, about withdrawing from school, about when tuition payments are due, and when financial aid checks are available. Mark all important dates in your planner or PDA. Carry your planner or PDA with you.

Fortunately, today, much of this information is now accessible online. Go to the college's website, and learn how to navigate to get to the resources that you will need. Which links take you to information about class schedules and registration? Where are the faculty pages where you can get email addresses, phone numbers, office locations, and office hours? What additional resources are available so that you can access those at any time, from any place?

Reading about the logistical details of college life would certainly rank low on the list of the most intellectually liberating and stimulating tasks in college, but it will surely help you get through the bureaucracy of college life. And, that's by no means an insignificant task—so don't fight it. Read the rules, figure out the rules, and learn all the angles and exceptions to the rules so that you know how to use them to benefit your educational experience. Then, get on with the good stuff, and start having some fun learning.

2. Visit Your Academic Advisor Often

Whether your college assigns students to a specific advisor, provides group or drop-in advising, or allows you to make appointments with a designated group of advisors, take advantage of this very important service. Think of academic advisors as coaches. A coach's goal is to help you grow, improve your skills, prepare you for each upcoming challenge, and achieve your goals.

In community college, the academic advisor's primary purpose is to help you succeed in your academic work. The advisor's service and advice are free. And you can—and should—work closely with one advisor if possible, rather than using drop-in services. At some colleges, you can change your academic advisor if you don't believe the advisor is the right fit for you and your needs. What more could you ask for?

Like a coach, the academic advisor is not only looking out for you but is also responsible for helping you to follow the institutional rules. Advisors will help you to keep track of the requirements you have completed and those you still need to complete. If your grades are slipping or if you are in academic trouble, your advisor will want to talk with you about what you can do and options that you have for ensuring your success.

Because some students view the academic advisor as the gatekeeper and rule enforcer or as the person who intervenes only when academic difficulties arise, they maintain some distance from advisors' offices. Others choose to wait until they have completed a lot of credits before they see an advisor. Both approaches are mistakes. Academic advisors want students to succeed academically and graduate from college. Their goal is not to make problems for you but to help you reach your educational goals.

Your advisor can give you tips on good classes to take. Advisors constantly hear from students about the teaching approaches of different instructors. They are tremendous resources. Ask them lots of questions to get the information that you feel you need to know.

What advisors like best is to think together with you about your intellectual interests, professional goals, and life commitments. They want to help you chart your own path but want you to make the decisions about what course to take or path to choose. Advisors can help you think about possible majors, about prerequisites you need to complete, and even about the differences in programs at the various four-year colleges in your areas. Advisors can also help you prepare to enter the workforce in your new profession.

It's your education, and you must make your own choices. However, community colleges provide you with a great resource in the form of academic advisors. They know a great deal of information that will help you make your way, and they are at your service free of charge, as often as you'd like. Be sure to take advantage of this great resource!

3. Go to Office Hours

It is important for you to meet and talk one-on-one with your community college instructors and, if possible, to do so during office hours. Some students are wary about going to office hours. You may feel intimidated about having a one-on-one discussion with college instructors. You might wonder why your instructors would want to spend their time talking with you when they have lectures to prepare, papers to grade, and other colleagues to talk with. If your instructor teaches part-time at your college, he or she might not even have designated office hours. However, you should make the effort to meet and talk with your instructor, even if you must do so right before or after class.

Many students go to office hours right after an exam to complain about their grades or to get help with what went wrong. It's reasonable to talk with your instructor about these issues, and you should definitely ask about what you didn't understand on an exam. However, as a general rule, if that's the only time you visit, it's not likely to lead to a stronger relationship. Some students come to their instructor just prior to an upcoming exam or paper. That's also a good time to speak with your instructor. The only difficulty may be that if you come just before the assignment due date, you're likely to be rushed through your meeting because you'll be waiting in line with lots of your classmates. Once again, visiting your instructor to discuss an upcoming assignment can be helpful to you, but it won't likely be a relationship builder.

The best time to visit office hours or to email or sign up for an appointment is during those times in the term when there is no imminent paper or exam. You should come prepared to ask and talk about any questions you have about the course or the readings or topics. If you have some background on the topic, share that with the instructor. You might also want to ask the instructor about his or her broader interest and experience in the field. Find out more about what your instructors' interests are and what projects they're currently working on.

You'll likely find that your instructor will help guide the office hour discussion and will take an interest in you. Even if it doesn't seem that way at first, you might be surprised one day when the instructor stops you on the way out of class and follows up on your earlier conversation. Yes, she really was listening! If you go back to her office that week or the week after (and if you are always courteous about keeping or, if necessary, cancelling appointments), you're likely to have twice the impact and twice the possibility of building an ongoing relationship.

All instructors were college students themselves, and part of what they appreciate about their lives as community college teachers is the opportunity to engage with interested and interesting students, just like you.

4. Find and Use the Resources to Help You Succeed

Every now and then we are surprised to hear a student state that he or she did not come to office hours or seek outside help with an assignment because that seemed like the wrong thing to do. Instead of getting help, students sometimes struggle, sometimes making the same mistake from assignment to assignment, or trying different but ineffective strategies for understanding a particularly difficult concept.

Students choose not to seek help for a number of reasons. Some have a kind of "do-it-on-my-own" attitude—they believe they should learn totally on their own, without any assistance at all from peers, from instructors, or from anyone. They feel that if they ask for help, they are somehow not really doing the work. Others put off getting help, figuring that if they just keep trying, ideas or answers or solutions will suddenly appear. Some students don't even know that their campus has resources just for them.

Smart students, however, learn about all of the support that is available to them, and they use it. Some of the most important resources available to you are your instructors. Ask questions in class and during office hours. Sometimes asking a question early can save you lots of frustration as well as hours of effort.

You should also carefully check your course syllabus to see what additional resources have been identified for supporting student learning for that course. Most colleges offer tutoring services, particularly for math and English. But community colleges recognize that there are other disciplines in which many, if not most, students could use additional help. For this reason, they offer tutoring in biology, medical terminology, and physics. Tutors might be instructors or other students who have already successfully completed courses in that area. Some colleges also provide online access to tutors.

Other kinds of support include open labs or centers, support courses, and workshops in areas like math, writing, or the sciences. These centers are usually staffed by instructors or have them on call to help students. Many students have found that taking a course or attending a workshop about math anxiety or college success skills has helped them develop strategies for improving their success in their courses.

Many colleges also offer support for particular groups of students. For example, your community college might have a veterans' office, a women's program, disability support services, and programs for students who are first generation or low income. It might have outreach programs for certain career paths, for instance, in nursing or in science and health technologies. Many of these programs provide individual counseling support, tutoring, and a sense of community with other students and faculty.

Finally, if you know—or suspect—that you have a disability, by all means, make an appointment with the Disability Support office on your campus to arrange for the appropriate support to help your learning. You should know that in college students have the responsibility to provide documentation of their disabilities and to identify the kind of help that they need, whether it is for a non-distracting test-taking environment, a note-taker, or the opportunity to sit close to the front of the class. Don't wait for your professors to figure out what you need; obtaining accommodations is *your* responsibility. Of course, some students with disabilities feel that they need to prove to themselves that they can succeed entirely on their own, without accommodation. Instead of letting their professors know some of the simple steps that would ensure their success, they wait too long, which makes it harder for them to catch up. Don't wait. Request accommodation early enough to give your professors time to make the arrangements that will help you to do your very best work.

Smart professional athletes know they can improve their performance by working with coaches who can help them with their batting stance or their golf swing. For the same reason, like all smart students, you should use all of the resources available to you to help you improve your academic performance.

5. Take the Right Credit Load and Course Sequences for You

One of the most important steps you can take is to determine the right credit load for you and your circumstances. The "right" credit load may change from term to term and over the course of your studies. You may find that it works best for you to start with one or two courses and work up to full time. Or you may find that you need to shift between taking a full credit load and attending school part-time, depending on the season and term. Always keep in mind, however, that what is right for others is not necessarily right for you. Your credit load will be right only if works for your situation and your needs. What factors should you consider to make the best decision?

First, carefully analyze how much time your job, family, athletic, or other co-curricular responsibilities already require. Remember to add in time for sleeping and eating and recreation. Don't forget to account for what you least expect—an illness, a work emergency, traffic jam, or car breakdown. Use this information to determine how much unscheduled time you actually have. Are there potential schedule conflicts? Will shift changes at work or an away game schedule conflict with lab hours? Are there adjustments you can make?

If you are able to meet with an academic or program advisor to plan your schedule, ask how much time students usually need for reading, homework, and studying to succeed in the classes you intend to take. When you are first starting or enrolling in the most challenging courses, use the high-end figure to make your decisions. If your advisor says students in introductory biology need two to three hours of out-of-class study time for each hour of class, use the higher number to calculate your time. For a five-credit class, this means you would need to plan for five hours of class sessions plus fifteen hours for reading, reviewing your notes, meeting with a study group or your professor, and writing up your lab results. For an online course, you might need to plan more time. With the demands on your time, can you manage the twenty hours a week it will take you to succeed in this one course?

If you decide that you can allow enough time to succeed in a particular course, your next question is whether you can manage another course like it or whether you should balance your load with a class that is less demanding.

Since some community colleges do not identify the skill sets that are needed to succeed in particular courses, you also want to work closely with your advisor to determine the right sequence of courses. Perhaps the description of the biology course you need for your nursing program includes a recommendation of proficiency in chemistry. You should take this recommendation very seriously. If you have never taken chemistry, ask your advisor which chemistry class you should take. If it has been a long time since you passed high school chemistry, you should ask your advisor if you should take a refresher class first. When you do enroll in that biology class, you want to be prepared with the knowledge and skills it takes to succeed. While good learners do learn from their failures, they should also learn to avoid unnecessary failures.

There are other factors to consider. If you are receiving financial aid or support from a retraining program, you may need to enroll in enough credits to continue to receive support. You may also need to ensure that the courses you take meet particular requirements. Your advisor can help you review your options and develop a flexible plan.

You might want to consider taking courses in summer term. While summer can be a time to clear your head and rest or perhaps work additional hours, it might also be a good time to enroll in a course that serves as a prerequisite for a course you need or want to take. You might consider taking a course you have avoided because you aren't sure how well you will do. Summer classes have a different feel than courses during the regular academic term. If you take just one or two classes, having the additional time to focus on a challenging course can help reduce your anxiety about taking it.

Finally, if you find during a term that you are taking more credits than you can manage successfully, by all means, meet with your advisor to evaluate your options. Should you discuss the possibility of an incomplete with your professor? Should you withdraw from a class? If so, which one?

You have made a choice to change your life. While it is important to complete your education, you will want to make sure that you keep your long-range goals in mind. Future employers and the selection committees who review transfer applications are more concerned with good transcripts than they are with how quickly students completed their degrees. Remember, it is most important that you succeed in your courses, even if you must do so slowly.

6. Anticipate and Prepare for Emergencies

Have you ever seen handouts that outline steps people can take for emergency preparedness? There are emergency kits for cars, emergency guidelines for people who are heading into the wilderness, and emergency plans for people who live in flood or earthquake zones. As strange as this might sound, we sometimes feel that it's a good idea for college students to review their own emergency preparedness.

All of us, including instructors, sometimes begin the new term in each year as though everything will go perfectly: copiers will always be available, computers will work without a single breakdown, the lab and library will always be open and the Internet accessible and, of course, no one will get ill.

This is seldom the case. While we would love for you to have a completely crisis-free community college experience, we think it's not a bad idea for you to plan what you would do in case problems do arise.

You probably know this already, but the most common emergencies seem to arise when we procrastinate. Almost everyone knows that we never seem to need an emergency plan more than when a paper is due or an exam is scheduled. That's why, if there were such a thing as an emergency kit for community college students it would include items such as stress remedies, back-ups for electronic copies of schoolwork, extra ink for printers, and lots of paper. Some students also need to include very loud alarm clocks, and maybe more than one.

But even if we could put together the best kit imaginable, it wouldn't be enough. Emergency preparedness also means having a plan. What will you do if you or a family member becomes ill or your child needs to be picked up from school while you are in class?

How will you learn what you need from a class you missed because an employee in your workplace is ill and you have to cover his or her shift? What steps will you take if the concept you thought you understood is no longer clear to you and the exam on it is this week? What if your roommate trips and dumps soup onto your laptop just as you are finishing the essay that is due tomorrow? What will you do if, on your way to give your final presentation, you are late to class because you are in a minor traffic accident? What if a small emergency turns into a long-term one?

This is where the steps you have been taking all term pay off. You have already formed study groups with other students in your class. You have the phone numbers and email addresses of your most reliable peers. You have met your instructors during office hours. You have established your own reliability and sense of purpose in class for your peers and your instructors. You know whom you can trust for class notes or an opportunity to review material for an exam or paper. You know who will pick up course materials for you. You know whether this emergency can be solved by a quick phone call or email or whether you need to meet in person with your instructor to discuss options.

Most important of all, because you have prepared, you can remain calm and focused. You can assess your situation, make good critical decisions, and develop alternative plans for doing what you need to do to succeed.

7. Work Out Win-Win Arrangements with Your Instructors and Your Employer

It can happen: you have a carefully planned schedule that balances your job, family, and class schedule. You have worked with your advisor to establish a plan for how you will meet your degree requirements to graduate on time. Then your co-workers need to trade shifts or your workforce supervisor or your employer increases your hours or reschedules them in a way that conflicts with your class or study time. Now what?

Sometimes you can work additional hours or a different schedule and still achieve your goals. Sometimes the additional income is welcome. But what if these changes affect your studies? Do you have any alternative other than to accept lower grades or to withdraw from one or more classes?

You should never be afraid to ask your employer for a meeting to discuss alternatives. You may be surprised to discover that your employer is one of the many in this country who values the importance of a college education. Of course, do not expect your employer to solve your problem. Instead, use your negotiation skills to develop a proposal that you think can benefit everyone.

You will want to think carefully about your work situation, your employer's needs, your co-workers' needs, and your own needs. Is there any flexibility in the schedule? Are there opportunities to trade work times? Once you understand the work rhythms of the school term, you might be able to negotiate shifts with co-workers or your employer. Can you work additional hours during your term break or during the slower part of the term in order to have adequate time for study during midterms and finals?

Similarly, negotiate with your instructors, but don't expect them to come up with solutions for your situation either. Most will be willing to discuss the situation, however. In fact, no matter what the outcome, make sure that you explain your situation to your instructors. They also want you to succeed. They will be particularly receptive if you come to them with a well-developed plan for success. If a change in hours at your job affects your ability to attend part of a class or to miss a few classes, you can ask your instructor to consider your plan for ensuring that you will keep up with the coursework. You might arrange additional study group sessions with your classmates, or ask if you can get assignments in advance so you can use your days off to prepare for class. Remember that instructors also have in mind the success of all of their students, so your plan will be more effective if you have considered not just your own needs but also those of your instructors and classmates.

If you cannot negotiate a solution, consider alternatives. Your decision about these alternatives will depend on your financial circumstances as well as your long-term goals. But before you decide, think carefully about your investments. If it is at all possible, consider working fewer hours, at least for a term or two, in order to do your very best in the courses you have already paid for in terms of tuition, books, and time. Keep in mind your long-term goals and priorities. You may find it easier to consider short-term sacrifices if those help you get where you want to be five years from today.

8. Don't Freak Out over Finals

You've taken tests and written papers throughout twelve or more years of prior schooling. You may have also done so as part of training for the military or for your job. In all likelihood, you've also taken final exams before. If you take a moment to think about it, you have as much experience in test taking as you do in almost any aspect of your life. Consider yourself an expert!

As the last weeks of the term approach, there's always a buzz on campus about finals. "How many finals do you have?" "Are they spaced out over several days or bunched together?" "I hear that instructor gives really hard finals." "I have only one final, but I've got three long papers due." "I've got to get at least a B on my final to get a decent grade." Rise above this unfortunate level of anxiety that spreads through campus.

You know how to do this. Make a finals schedule, a study guide for each class, and a study schedule. Figure out where you want to study—your room, the library, a lounge, an empty classroom. Arrange for study groups or prepare by yourself. Review your notes and texts and identify key themes, topics, and information. Stay healthy by eating right and getting enough sleep. Reserve some free time to relax. Get to the exam a few minutes early, take a deep breath, complete the final, and give a sigh of relief.

If it's that easy, why does it seem so hard? The hardest part is psychological. While there is an elevated level of anxiety on campus about finals, it is still within normal limits. But, the anxiety can become unhealthy.

What you need to remember is that a final exam is just an exam. Be smart by anticipating that there may be a heightened degree of anxiety among your classmates. Know that it's coming, but don't let it affect you. Focus on your studies, not the anxieties in the air. Eat well. Get rest. Avoid the all-nighter if at all possible. However, if you should feel overwhelmed at any point, go to the campus counseling office where there are almost always extra staff on duty, walk-in appointments, and people ready to assist and support you at this point in the term. Finals go by very quickly, and before you know it, you'll be done and ready for a few days of work, rest, relaxation, and a much-needed change of pace.

9. Plan for Enrollment, Tuition, and Other Deadlines

One of the most surprising aspects of community college is the complexity of schedules. You may have already figured out how to balance your work, life, and class schedule, but there is another layer that is very important. Colleges have complex and confusing schedules, and you need to learn about the important dates, enrollment periods, and deadlines at your school.

In addition to planning carefully for the term in which you are enrolled—start times for the term and for your classes, the final day of classes, the exam week schedule—plan almost simultaneously for the next one. The registration period for an upcoming term or semester usually occurs at some point after midterm. To make sure you are able to get the classes that you want and need, enroll on time. In addition to marking the enrollment period in your planner, you should note the advising period, so you can contact your advisor to schedule an appointment prior to the enrollment period. Your advisor will not only help you plan which classes to take, he or she can also let you know if those classes tend to fill quickly. You definitely do not want to miss out on a good class because you neglected to keep these important dates in mind.

There are other important dates as well. You should be familiar with your college's policy about adding and dropping classes. Many colleges have an "open" period during which you can add or drop a class without a fee or formal permission when you need to make changes in your schedule.

You also need to know your community college's tuition refund policy. If you need to withdraw from a class early in the term, your school may permit a full or partial refund of your tuition. Don't get caught dropping a course too late to get your refund! Check to see if there is a deadline for being able to withdraw on your own.

At some community colleges, after a certain point in the term, you might need your instructor's permission for a hardship withdrawal.

If your community college permits you to sign up on a waiting list for a course, familiarize yourself with how that works. Will you be moved automatically into the course if a space opens or do you need to speak to the instructor? Will you be notified? Will you be charged tuition if you were moved into the class automatically but didn't realize it?

If you are applying for or receiving financial aid, record those deadlines in your planner, too. You don't want to waste valuable time because you forgot to ask for a signature that is required before you can receive payments for purchasing textbooks.

Finally, know the tuition deadlines. This information will help you plan your budget and make sure that you submit your payment on time.

4

Management Fundamentals: Balance Responsibilities of Family, Work, and Daily Life

1. Be Clear about Your Goals and Priorities

You have many responsibilities as a college student. As a result, you need to be particularly careful about conflicts that can arise during a term. You will be happy to know that most schedule conflicts can be avoided with careful attention to the schedule of classes and exams and the course syllabi. However, when a conflict does arise and you cannot reschedule, you always have the option of discussing the situation with your instructors. If you have a plan for ensuring that you stay caught up with the coursework, you might find that you can resolve the problem.

At times you will need to weigh your options carefully to make the best choice. Being clear about your short-term and long-term priorities can help. If you are torn between driving to class or staying home for an extra day to recuperate from an illness, weigh your options. If staying home one additional day allows you to perform better the rest of the term, then you should stay home.

Eventually, however, you might be faced with a more difficult decision. You might have a conflict about whether you should attend class or meet with your child's teacher. Or perhaps you have the opportunity to be sent by your workforce supervisor or employer to a training session that improves your chances for promotion. What should you do? If you evaluate the situation in terms of your clearly articulated goals, you will be able to reach a decision that is reasonable for you.

Consider these two students' dilemmas. One student, a single parent, was torn between preparing for a final exam and attending her child's school play. She decided that finishing her course with a good grade was more important in the long run so that she could meet her long-term goal of providing financial security for her and her son. As disappointed as she was to miss this one play, she decided that there would be other school plays.

Another student found out part way through his fall term that his grandfather, who lived in another state, was dying and needed care. He decided to withdraw from his classes in order be with his grandfather and help provide care. While he valued his schooling and had clear goals about succeeding, he reasoned that he could enroll in another term, but that he would not have another chance to spend time with his grandfather.

Being clear about your priorities doesn't mean that you will necessarily find it easy to choose. It also doesn't mean that you will like the alternatives. It does mean, however, that you will find it easier to live with the choices that you make.

2. Use a Planner to Manage Your Time Effectively

Two of the most important skills you absolutely need to develop are organization and time management. Why? If, like many students, you are working 25 or more hours a week, you will have to figure out ways to use your time efficiently. If you have just completed (or are still in) high school, you will discover that, unlike high school, in community college you are responsible for keeping track of all that you do. In either case, unless you know how to organize yourself and your day, you will easily and quickly get lost.

Your first step should be to establish a system for keeping track of the work for each course that you do. This includes syllabi, assignments, due dates, and work that you submit and receive back. You should always have a copy of the syllabus for each course. It is your guide to expectations and requirements. You should also save graded work that is returned to you, at a minimum until final grades are posted. We recommend that you keep the work even longer in case you transfer to a four-year college that requires that you submit a portfolio of your community college work, including material from English (ESL, developmental, and writing), math, and science classes.

Most important, you will need to be organized in terms of your time. Many students don't understand that community college is very different in terms of routines. Classes may start at a different time every day, and there will be breaks during the day when you will need to study, meet with faculty during their office hours, or get together with friends. You may have night classes, study groups, or a work schedule to remember. You may need to coordinate your schedule with your spouse's work hours or your children's day care. In your online classes, you will be completely responsible for keeping track of assignments, participating as required in discussions, and meeting due dates. Be sure to allow time for possible delays in communications from your classmates and instructor. And if this is the first time you are on your own, away from home, remember that no one will be checking to see that you get to class on time or remind you to attend a meeting where people are counting on you to be there.

Of course, although many schools and community colleges in recent years have encouraged students to regularly use planners or PDAs, many students still resist. Sometimes the resistance comes from feeling too busy to take time to write down appointments and schedules. That's a sure sign that you need one.

Another reason some people don't use planners is because they don't believe their schedule is complicated or that they need a reminder to keep track of their lives. But a planner can help you discover your commitments and to prioritize them. We often ask students in our classes to estimate the time they spend on various activities and how much time they actually need, including time for studying. The students fill out a daily activity monitor for just one week—including time to commute, shop for groceries, exercise, help their children with math homework, and revise and type their papers. Most are surprised by how much time it takes to meet all of their commitments.

A planner, whether electronic or paper, can help you to meet your most important commitments, and reduce your stress level. The first step is to make a schedule for each day, each week, and each month. Then you need to write the times of all your commitments, including classes, work hours, exercise routines, extracurricular activities, and appointments. Write in due dates for assignments and exams, registration periods for the next term, deadlines for tuition—any dates that could be important.

Fill in the unstructured time with estimates for study time, commuting, recreation, sleep, extracurricular activities, social functions, and even just hanging out. Only you will know, and it may even take you some time to discover, how your plans work best in terms of balancing effective study and social time. Do you need to study in short blocks so that an hour between classes becomes a powerful study time when you can get a great amount accomplished? Or do you require three- to four-hour-long uninterrupted blocks of time to really focus on a topic? Maybe you need some of both to account for different kinds of assignments.

Hopefully, you will have organized your schedule and learned to manage your time so that you are comfortable about handling all the competing demands on your time. As you learn about your study needs, make sure you revise your schedule so that it allocates plenty of time to complete your assignments well but also keeps you balanced personally and socially. You will need both, and you will need limits on both so that you remain a well-rounded person.

Because you have so much responsibility for your schedule, and your schedule will be so full and varied, allow a planner to give you a little support to manage your life. After all, you are the one who is scheduling your exciting and very full life, so you don't want to miss out on all that you have planned.

3. Establish a Routine for Schoolwork

Whether you live alone or with your family or roommates, you will want to establish a routine for yourself for reading, homework, and doing assignments. As you probably already know, having a set routine—even if that routine is not identical day to day—helps make sure you complete the most important tasks without becoming distracted by other, often wonderful, ways to spend your time.

First, find a place that works for you when you are studying alone. It might be your bedroom or a study. It might be someplace on campus. You may have to experiment a bit to figure out the best place. Many students find that having a television or music nearby while they study proves too distracting. Others have found that they cannot study when there is complete silence. A few have noted, quite ruefully, that they are more likely to stay awake if they study anywhere except on top of their beds.

In addition to having a good place for your studies, you need to figure out the best time. This of course should be a time during which you are alert, able to read, and take notes efficiently and with the fewest distractions. You may be the kind of person who studies best with a long, uninterrupted block of time. Or you may prefer a kind of punctuated rhythm to your studies, alternating reading or working on homework problems with short breaks for more physical activity.

When you sit down to study, the first thing to do is get yourself organized. Review your assignments. What is due the next day, the next week, the next month? How much time is needed for each assignment? Which assignment are you mentally and physically prepared to focus on first, so that the most difficult assignment will have your deepest concentration? Know whether your study style is to immerse yourself in a single project for hours at a time or to work in 20- or 30-minute chunks. Pace yourself. Plan breaks.

When you form a study group, you will be negotiating with the other members of your group about times and place. You are likely to find that coordinating a whole group's schedule requires quite a bit of patience and skill. The solutions groups develop are as varied as you could ever imagine. Some students reserve study rooms in the library for sessions right before or right after class. Some students locate empty classrooms or arrange a combination of face-to-face and electronic meetings. Perhaps you can find a coffee shop midway between all of your homes where you can study and peer review your essays.

Whatever routines you establish, make sure that they are effective and that they allow you to complete your work and have it fresh in mind for your next class.

4. Learn to Negotiate to Help You Study and Achieve Academically

One of the most valuable skills you possess as a community college student is your ability to negotiate effective compromises. In fact, your ability to negotiate effective solutions for dilemmas that you encounter is important in almost every aspect of your life—in your relationships with your family and friends.

So how does negotiation help you as a student? If you have roommates, chances are that your schedules and personal rhythms don't match. You may find that you like a quiet space for study while one or more of your roommates likes music or that when you most need to take time off and celebrate they need quiet time. If you have children, you may discover that an independent family member suddenly becomes needy when you have homework or a project to complete.

Rather than accept a frustrating situation or allow your resentment to build, seek solutions that help everyone. Negotiate with your roommates to establish a balance of quiet and social times. You might want to work closely with your spouse to alternate responsibility for picking up or dropping off children at day care. You do not need to be the person who does everything at home: you can share household chores with other family members. If you already share, you can trade out times and do less during exam week in exchange for doing more during the term break. You might want to try a strategy used by one student who was very frustrated because her two young sons didn't understand that she needed lots of quiet time to write papers. In order to complete her research course, she negotiated a deal for two quiet hours every morning in exchange for taking her sons to the place of their choice to play in the afternoons.

You can use these chances to hone your negotiation skills. Assume the best, that you will all benefit from working cooperatively to find solutions. Think about different ways to explain your own situation and needs clearly and honestly. Learn to listen carefully and respectfully to others when they explain theirs. When you listen, you will be able to hear and understand the other person's needs. And this will enable you to think creatively about options that can meet everyone's needs.

At times you may be tempted to give in to an unsatisfactory situation rather than to take the time to address it. But you should ask whether doing that would really help you to meet your goals. While you will not always be able to completely solve any and all dilemmas, with intelligence, skills, and a good measure of creativity, you can often negotiate solutions that help you to meet your goals. And one of the wonderful outcomes will be the joy you share with family and friends who feel that they have been an important part of your success.

5. Create Space for Yourself

As you juggle all of your responsibilities—taking difficult classes, working twenty or more hours a week, participating in extracurricular activities or doing volunteer work, nurturing your relationships with your family and friends, keeping your household somewhat organized—you may find yourself overwhelmed.

What you are learning and accomplishing can seem to give you boosts of energy. But over a long and sustained period, you may find yourself increasingly anxious or just plain "out of gas." As strange as it may sound, you also need to pay attention to yourself and your own needs.

One of most important steps you can take is to create a space and a time that are just for you. The physical space could be a room or a corner of a room, a yoga mat or a park or trail, a carrel in the library, or even the front seat of your car. It may be a space that you use primarily for studying, but you should also use it for being alone. Choosing to be in your space gives you time to pause and reflect. It gives you time to wind down, to relax, to reevaluate, to think, and to contemplate the world. It allows you to do nothing.

During your personal time, you may choose to listen to music or make music. You may choose to be completely quiet. You might go for a walk. You might just lie in your bed and close your eyes, or stare up at the ceiling. You can review the past day, your relationships, your classes, your conversations. You can watch TV. You can go to a movie. You can go to an event on campus by yourself. You can eat a meal by yourself. You can do nothing.

Sometimes the act of doing nothing allows you to do the most. This reflective time can free the clutter from your mind so that you can think clearly. Sometimes silence is necessary to allow you to hear yourself think. Sometimes closing your eyes allows you to see more clearly than ever before. Sometimes being alone will help you be an even better companion to those you care about and like to be around.

Making time to find your own inner voice will help you as a college student. More important, it will help you to develop ways to sustain your own energy over longer periods of times and to discover one of your very best lifelong friends.

6. Don't Fall Behind: Be Both the Tortoise and the Hare

Time will play tricks with your mind at the start of college. You may think that you have loads of free time for studying. You may be surprised in the first weeks of the term that some instructors are reviewing material you remember from high school. You will take heart that only a few papers are required in any given social science or humanities course over the entire term.

"What's the big deal?" you will think. College does not seem as difficult as you always heard. Instead of studying, you may choose to increase your hours at work or to fill your time with extracurricular activities, clubs, socializing, or watching lots of TV.

Then all of a sudden, the pace will change dramatically. The first exams will be held. The first set of papers will be due. Instead of review, your instructors will begin covering new material two or three times as fast as you ever studied anything before. In each class you will be reading one or more long chapters in a week and several high-level academic articles for each class session.

How will you keep up when the academic term shifts into warp speed? The answer is simple. You will need to have the best traits of both the tortoise and the hare. You need to be steady and consistent, like the turtle, ready for the long haul of the academic term. At the same time, you need to be ready, like the rabbit, for the bursts of energy required when there is an especially heavy load of tests or papers in any given week. You definitely want to make sure that you have the energy for a strong finish. So it's best to keep yourself in good mental and physical health for those times when you need to set everything aside to get all your work done.

The key is to always keep up with your work, even when the workload seems light. Falling behind and catching up later should not be an option. Trust us on this one—it won't work. By keeping up with your work, you will be in good shape when a rush of assignments from multiple classes are all due at once. It will allow you flexibility for those times when you catch a cold, have heavy extracurricular commitments, or a very exciting opportunity comes up spontaneously.

Keep in mind that generations of students have been able to keep up with the heavy workload. You have all the intellectual ability and experience not only to keep up but to excel in all your subjects. Just remember to be both the tortoise and the hare, and don't let yourself fall behind.

7. Think Sensibly and Strategically about Grades

How should you think about grades in college? Will college be a repeat of how you performed in high school?

Let's first do the mathematics of community college grades. In a traditional semester system at a community college, you would take an average of four courses each term, attend two semesters each year, and go for two years in preparation for an associate in arts in a trade/profession or a transfer degree to a four-year school. That comes to sixteen classes. In a quarter system, you might take three courses for each of three quarters over two years for a total of eighteen classes. Thus, the final grade for each class you take counts for only about 6 percent of your final community college grade point average. In each class, you will have an average of four assignments or exams that comprise your grade. If each of these assignments were weighted equally, then each would be worth approximately 1.5 percent, of your final community college grade point average.

Keep these calculations in mind when you get your first grades on papers or tests in your first term at college. If you get the first C of your career on your first exam—and many students do get lower-than-expected grades on their first papers and exams—use it as a learning experience about college expectations for quality of work and the necessity of good study skills. But don't panic about it being a career-ending signal. That C you received counted only 1.5 percent of your final GPA. It didn't rule you out for a career in health care, law enforcement, or teaching or for further studies in biology or sociology.

Some students vociferously argue about getting a B– grade rather than a B. If you think your instructor made a mathematical error or some other clear and legitimate mistake in your grade, bring it to his or her attention. Otherwise, just forget about it.

Relax. A B– grade means you did good work in that course. Feel good about your accomplishment.

You might think you deserve an A on a paper because your high school teacher praised your writing, unlike your community college instructor, who has numerous suggestions on how you can improve. Please don't complain. What you need to do, instead, is adjust your expectations and raise your own standards.

If you believe you need an A to get a scholarship or be accepted into a four-year college, don't think your sense of entitlement will go very far with your instructor. Instead, seek out guidance for how to do better.

This does not mean that grades are not important. If you are receiving financial aid, you must, of course, maintain good grades. If you are applying to transfer to a four-year college, your GPA will certainly be one of the important admissions criteria. However, most universities take a number of factors into account. Faculty letters of reference, courses in your intended major, experience or special accomplishments in your intended field, and community service will often carry considerable weight in conjunction with the more traditional measures. If you plan to go out and look for a job after you receive your associate's degree, few employers will look closely or exclusively at your grade point average.

It is true that transfer students need to keep their overall grade averages in mind. Clearly, those who graduate with a 3.5 GPA or higher are in a stronger position than those who graduate with a 2.5 GPA or lower. In this sense, grades do matter. But they shouldn't matter to the extent that you focus on them more than you focus on learning or that you lose any of the joy of the community college experience for the achievement of a high grade point average. Further, they shouldn't cause you to worry endlessly about any single low grade you receive.

Think about how you want to approach the issue of grades in college. Most important, focus on your learning.

8. Be Careful about Finances

Credit cards are not free money. They are not birthday gifts from a bank. They represent *your* money, and every dollar *you* spend, *you* will have to repay, often with high interest.

Credit cards, when used properly, are perfectly fine and provide an excellent alternative to carrying cash or checks with you. The problem is that some people—especially young college students— misuse credit cards. Anyone can be tempted to rely on credit to cover some of the expenses of their college education. The challenge is to manage your credit carefully and not to abuse it.

First, ask the bank to set a low credit limit to help you from overspending. Second, only spend money "on credit" that you have set aside in your budget to spend. You never want to pay credit card interest rates. Interest rates are what ruin financial futures. You gain the advantage over the banks if you spend only an amount that you can pay off in full with every monthly bill.

If this is the first time you've had a credit card, you may be tempted by the opportunity to go online or into a store to make purchases without paying cash, just credit. That's the trap that far too many people (especially young college students) fall into—be sure to avoid it. If you don't have the money to pay for an item, don't buy it. The second trap is that you are likely to forget today what you purchased on your credit last week or even yesterday and, as a result, your monthly bill might shock you.

Bank checks and debit cards would seem to be much more simple. You have put money in the bank and opened a checking account in your own name. You write checks and use your debit card, you keep track of the checks and debit charges you've made in your check ledger or online, and you balance your statement on a regular basis. But sometimes what seems simple in theory isn't so simple in practice.

Carefully monitoring your checking balance will help you manage your spending and avoid bounced checks, high fees for those bounced checks, and potential problems with credit. Be sensible and attentive in your use of credit/debit cards and bank checks. Use credit cards wisely, as if they were cash in your pocket, and always pay on time. Remember to record and balance your checkbook each time you write a check, use your debit card, or have an electronic withdrawal. If you even think you might have a problem paying your bills, get help immediately from family, community college counselors, your credit card company, and the bank.

9. Make Homework a Family Activity

Raising children while going to college presents some very interesting challenges. As every parent knows, children's needs seldom follow predictable schedules. We know students who, partway through their first term, have found themselves wondering why they ever thought they could continue to meet all their responsibilities as a parent and still do well in their community college courses. Remarkably, they have gone on to teach us that raising children while going to school presents not just challenges but wonderful opportunities as well.

First, your children are often the constant and visible reminders of why you have chosen to go to community college. Despite some frustrating moments, their presence reminds you of your goals and motivates you to succeed. It also reminds you that the sacrifices that you are all making together will help you to reach your goal of providing a better life for all of you.

Of course, once your children are in school themselves, they are also the ones who might best understand the pressures you face with your homework, papers, and preparation for tests. This is why many of our students with school-age children have said that they schedule at least some of their homework time with their children. If you haven't tried this already, do it soon. Sit side-by-side, reading and working on assignments. You may find that you can help each other. In exchange for some help on a math problem, your son might help you figure out how to set up a template on your computer for formatting your academic papers or practice assignments with you. Of course, if you are doing homework together, then you will also want to take breaks and together celebrate your accomplishments, too.

Doing homework with your children not only helps with the need for some quiet time; it also models good study habits. And, of course, it also seeds the idea of the importance of college and learning.

PART 3

A HIGH-QUALITY EDUCATIONAL EXPERIENCE

5

Beyond the Basics: Get a High-Quality College Education

1. Make Yourself Part of the Scholarly Community

Community college connotes different things to different people. We hope you'll be one of those students who thinks of college as a scholarly community in which you get to spend a few years of your life with a group of people who are deeply engaged with ideas, exploration, questioning, discovery, analysis, and problem solving. To do so will most definitely put you in the right mindset for a successful community college experience.

Consider for a moment some other ideas about college. We appreciate the fact that for some students, it is strictly a professional training ground where they are working on a certificate or credentials or are preparing for a career change. Still others think of it as a place of competition and endless judgment, tests, exams, and grades.

Why are you encouraged to approach your community college experience as a scholarly or professional community? Even if you are taking a single class, it's important to learn what you can from knowledgeable people in your field. As you continue your personal, social, professional, and intellectual growth, it's healthier to do so in a supportive environment of thinking, caring people.

Personal and social growth is, of course, essential, but what makes community college unique is the attention to analytic thinking, books, lectures, discussions, critical insights, discoveries, and information. You have the opportunity to be an active, contributing part of a collection of people, faculty, and students who are focused on learning, exploring, and thinking deeply about all sorts of issues and topics and inquiries. In terms of this aspect of community college, it's important that you begin to self-identify as a scholar or a scholar apprentice. This piece of advice is not intended to pigeonhole you or limit you socially; in fact, it will probably do just the opposite. It will prevent you from becoming overly parochial by allowing you to grow and expand exponentially.

Once you enter community college, it's actually very easy to become a part of the scholarly community. The hardest part is to make a shift in your mindset. Instead of thinking of coursework as a series of assignments, tests, and homework, think of it as a great opportunity for learning. Instead of thinking of your teachers as people who judge you and have control of grading, imagine them as mentors, fellow thinkers, senior colleagues, and scholarly friends and allies. Then look at bulletin boards or the school website to find different ways of joining the scholarly community. Attend guest lectures and talks on campus. Go to theater productions, art exhibits, and classical concerts. Read national and global newspapers. Peruse scientific and popular magazines that address intellectual issues. Visit instructors in their offices. Go to receptions, book signings, and poetry readings. Hang out with friends from your classes and talk about an exciting or controversial idea from your class that day.

2. Choose Good Instructors over Good Class Topics

Always choose the best instructor when you are planning your class schedule for the next term. Course topics and descriptions will catch your attention in college, and you will have hundreds of courses to choose from each term. Course topics are without a doubt important; however, a good instructor will always trump a good course title or description.

A good instructor will make any topic interesting and any course a worthwhile experience for you. You can get information and read about any topic or idea throughout your life. But a good instructor—or especially a great instructor—is a rare find, and you want to take full advantage of such an opportunity.

Good instructors force you to think and learn. They will be demanding of you, but they will be even more demanding of themselves. They will expect you to contribute to the success of the class and come to class prepared each day. They will be available and accessible to you, and they will be interested in what you are learning from the class.

Good instructors can be entertaining, but that's only occasionally the case. In fact, although you may want to sit back in lectures and be entertained, you should make a careful distinction between faculty who stand out as good entertainers and those who are good instructors. Good instructors will certainly help make learning interesting, stimulating, and enjoyable, but they may not be entertainers, and they will very likely require you to work and think very hard.

When you enroll in a course whose topic you like and whose description sounds interesting, you are likely to find it to be a great learning experience. But savvy students talk with their peers, other students, advisors, and even other instructors to find out more about who is teaching such an interesting topic. With good instructors, you will learn new content areas, you will be challenged to think deeply, and you will be asked to examine issues analytically and from multiple perspectives. You will be expected to do your best work, and you will want to do just that because of the high standards that the instructors hold for you and for themselves. You should take this opportunity to meet and to get to know these instructors through classroom interactions and during office hours.

If you enroll in a class with a good instructor teaching a course topic you're interested in, then you've hit the jackpot. Even for just that single course, you're going to have a terrific term. Count on it!

3. Find a Mentor

Everyone benefits from good mentoring. Mentors are people who take an interest in you as a coach, advisor, and supporter for your professional (and sometimes, personal) well-being. On occasion, a mentor may have a personal stake in your professional success, but he or she most often is simply looking out for your best interests. Mentors differ from parents, advisors, friends, instructors, and counselors, although these people may play roles similar to those of mentors.

When a mentor gives you advice, he or she will first and foremost know what your interests and strengths are and will always tailor the discussion very specifically to your individual needs. A mentor will guide you toward classes that will help you reach your degree and career goals. Mentors will let you know when there is a great opportunity for an internship or when special speakers are coming to campus. They will strategize with you when you face obstacles. They will listen to you when you are confused and thwarted. They will give you words of uplift and strength when you are feeling down, and they will help you figure out how to chart your course when you are ready to blaze new paths.

You have to take the initiative and responsibility to look for a mentor. Formal mentor programs are a good start for learning about the mentoring relationship. They offer you well-meaning people who will serve as a mentor in a formal role. At the same time, however, an assigned mentor will rarely support and coach you with the passion and commitment of someone in a mutually developed mentor relationship.

What you can do is try to develop relationships with people you respect and connect with at college. It's often as easy as following up on an instructor's comment of interest or praise about a paper you've written or a comment you've made in class. It can mean something as simple as visiting an instructor during his or her office hours to talk without having a very specific question or problem to present. Or, it could mean going to an instructor or staff person on campus when you do indeed have a problem and taking a risk to trust someone with your personal story.

Like all good relationships, mentoring takes time to develop and requires continuing nurturance. Good mentors will want time to get to know you and to determine whether they respect you as a person and as a professional. They will want to see the special spark of inner integrity and values that they admire. They will expect that you will be willing to share something about yourself. Mentoring relationships are ones of mutual respect and admiration. They involve generosity and giving. Be patient, and do not be demanding.

4. Pursue Your Intellectual Passions

Do you love to read historical novels? Could you spend hours conceptualizing and then tinkering with the mechanics of a science project or a diesel engine? Do you write poetry or do graphic arts in your free time? Are you consumed with a desire to learn more about environmental issues? Do you love to look at rock formations? Are you fascinated by the intersection of economics, international conflict, and ethnic hatred?

Dig deep into your life history to come up with a list of subjects that you've found fascinating, troubling, exciting, and just plain worth your time to think about. Begin to identify what you really care about and then find a way to pursue or at least explore these subject areas in college.

Many students are under the impression that they must immediately complete all of their core, distribution, or general education requirements. They feel considerable pressure to take a prescribed set of courses that they believe are required to advance them toward a particular profession or major or paraprofessional degree. This is particularly true for students in professional-technical programs, which often have extensive course requirements.

You may, however, have more flexibility for course choices than you imagine when you first enter community college. Yes, you do need to pay attention to program and/or general education or distribution requirements at your community college, and you should draft a plan of how you anticipate fulfilling all or many of those requirements in a timely manner. Most technical programs usually allow at least a few elective courses, and most transfer degrees have room for several. Keep in mind that employers and professional programs are much more open to applicants with a broad set of interests than most students imagine. Many law schools would love to have a few more philosophy majors. Many medical schools ask applicants to demonstrate their strengths in the humanities. Many businesses would love to hire bilingual workers.

Think of your personal list of favorite subjects, your passions, and interests as another set of requirements that you fulfill during community college, with equal standing to all the other requirements. You must effectively advocate for your personal set of requirements, your passions, and interests, and negotiate the other general education, major, and preprofessional requirements to create a balance in your course schedule and in your life. Be a strong advocate for your own set of favored requirements because this negotiation will be one of the decisive factors in determining whether you feel satisfied with your college education.

Remember, this is your education. Be true to yourself. This is the time in your life to explore those topics that excite you and to pursue those dreams that drive your intellectual passions.

5. Think Critically

It is the expectation that a college-educated person will think insightfully and analytically about issues and can get to the root of the complex questions and challenges that face us personally and as a society.

Thinking critically is one of the most essential lessons of college. Unfortunately, in high school, too few students are asked to think critically, even those who score very well on standardized tests, write well-organized essays on exams, and quickly complete advanced math assignments. Also, some supervisors value unquestioning adherence to procedures rather than independent thought.

Being a good critical thinker means that you are able to consider and analyze ideas, readings, debates, and discoveries in a comprehensive and thorough manner. It means that you can understand the nuances of an author's ideas and then cogently challenge those ideas. It means that you can understand a point of view and then critique that point of view from multiple perspectives. It means you can hold several compelling but competing ideas and arguments in your mind at the same time and then examine the strengths and weaknesses of each. It means that you're usually impatient with two-sided debates because you realize that most issues have more than two sides and that most issues are far more complex than the discussion that any debate format will elicit. It means that you ask difficult questions of yourself, others, and the physical world around you and that when you find reasonable answers to your questions, you ask a second and third set of questions that probe more broadly and more deeply.

Some of the supposedly best prepared students turn in first-term papers that are clear and well organized but unfortunately don't have much substance. The papers just don't say much. In high school students were praised and rewarded for such papers, but in college they will be expected to do much more. These papers have good form but insufficient substance and analysis. These students too often haven't been challenged to think critically. By contrast, we have other students whose paper writing skills are sometimes lacking, but in their lives they have somehow been forced to ask difficult questions and to analyze and challenge normative assumptions in deeper ways. In their papers, they are willing to explore challenging and meaningful ideas.

Both sets of students (of course, these groupings are overly broad generalizations) will have considerable work to do in college. The good news is that they all have the ability to think critically. The problem is that until college, few have been asked to do so.

If you had already finished your learning and intellectual development, you wouldn't need to be in college. Learning to think critically will permit you to lead and excel in so many personal, intellectual, civic, and professional fields. It's one of the greatest gifts of a good college education.

6. Be Part of a Learning Community

Community college students face a different set of challenges than students who attend residential colleges and universities. You are likely one of the majority of community college students who works either part-time or full-time and commutes, sometimes from a long distance, to get to classes. This does not mean, however, that you need to miss out on the opportunity to get to know instructors, meet them during their office hours, participate in study groups, meet after class to discuss class topics, and attend co-curricular lectures, speeches, and political debates. You should and certainly will have that opportunity, but you must be assertive to make sure it happens.

One of the best ways is to enroll, if possible, in one of the special academic programs offered at your community college. Many community colleges now offer course combinations called learning communities, and some offer them online. Some learning communities are part of honors programs. Some are designed to help students prepare for college-level work or for a specific major or profession. Although the purpose and label of learning community programs vary from college to college, these programs are recognizable because they offer students the chance to enroll in two or more courses taught together.

Learning communities, perhaps more than any other community college offering, emphasize the academic or scholarly community that can exist between faculty and students as part of the college experience. They provide a more efficient and convenient schedule. And they also provide an environment that supports academic success in which faculty and students engage with one another and build friendships around intellectual ideas and academic projects.

Learning communities are innovative, updated versions coming out of both the older and more traditional Oxford model and the alternative, democratic-based experimental colleges of the 1920s and 1930s and again in the 1960s. In a time in which community colleges and public universities can increasingly feel large and corporate-like, these programs hold onto the authentic and very best of college learning. Because they emphasize active learning and collaboration, learning communities give you a chance to meet and study with other students, instructors, and staff on a more personal basis. They can make learning coming alive!

At many community colleges, learning communities assign the same set of students to two or more classes or link instructors from different fields to team teach a single group of students in a way that creates intellectual connections between the different subjects. The integrative learning that occurs has proven to be a critical foundation for academic success. In addition, the opportunity to be in two or three classes with the same set of students allows for the development of the strong social connections that are so important to student success.

Some students worry that they will be limited by enrolling in a learning community. In our experience, it's very rare that community colleges set up programs that impose limits. These programs actually open doors to give you easy access to all the rich resources of the wider campus. These programs seek to get you more deeply engaged in campus activities than you would be if you did not participate in them.

If learning communities are offered in your college and you can choose to enroll in them, you should. These courses will enable you to take advantage of the very best educational experiences that colleges have to offer.

7. Take Advantage of High-Impact Learning Opportunities

In addition to learning communities, many colleges also offer programs that help students to create the kinds of strong bonds that support their learning and their enjoyment of the community college experience. These include small discussion classes, mentoring, honors programs, and study abroad opportunities.

In a small discussion class you participate as an active learner. You have the chance to present ideas, discuss readings, and engage with your teacher and fellow students in lively discourse. You learn how to engage with others who hold different viewpoints. You learn the important difference between the competitive debate model of discussion and the more collaborative form, intellectual inquiry.

The success of a small class depends as much on the quality of student participation as on the instructor's teaching qualities. Unlike most classes you've probably taken before, you carry a significant share of responsibility for class dynamics, the vibrancy of discussion, and the level of analytical thinking that takes place. When you do your work and come prepared to class, your peers and teacher all learn more deeply. You make a difference in the classroom.

Another important advantage of small classes is that you will have a chance to get to know an instructor in a close and personal way. You will get good insight into how this instructor thinks and how he or she approaches intellectual issues. You will develop a special relationship with this one particular instructor because of the regular, ongoing contact.

The small discussion class is the epitome of the college experience. There you are, with ten to twenty other intellectually curious students, exploring new ideas and perspectives with a community college instructor. You raise questions, voice opinions, present critical insights, and listen to the ideas and analyses of your peers and your instuctor. People in the room challenge each other to think more critically and explore the topic in greater depth.

In smaller discussion-oriented classes, your instructor guides you beyond surface understandings and interpretations to new and more complex understandings of topics. You realize that your intellectual capacity is much greater than you ever imagined. You are intellectually invigorated, and you and your classmates carry the class discussion into your thoughts and conversations throughout the day, continuing the conversation as you walk across campus after class.

Mentoring programs assign faculty, staff, and second-year students to an individual student or to groups of students to provide advice and support. Sometimes these mentors will take students to lunch or to a campus concert or invite them home for dinner and conversation.

Honors programs generally admit a select group of students, usually based on high school grades, and provide these students with greater academic challenges and the opportunity to take some courses together.

A chance to study or travel with a college in another country gives you the opportunity to both see how others live, and also to see your way of life, values, studies, and national and cultural society from an entirely different perspective. Your immersion in a new and different society allows you to grow and learn and see much more broadly than you could ever imagine. You are likely to encounter new cultures, values, and foods as well as different languages, news reports, economic systems, and governmental structures. You will find that people in other countries don't always view your world or way of life as the centerpiece of how they see the world and value life. Studying abroad can also prepare you well for a professional career that requires you to be culturally aware and sensitive to the perspectives and experiences of people living in different parts of the world.

You should definitely look into one or more of these special academic programs. One final benefit they provide is a unique opportunity to get to know your fellow college students. From your conversations in and out of class, you will learn about how each one thinks and how each one sees the world from a unique and special perspective. You will build close relationships with some of your classmates precisely because of your common classroom experience and the active, in-depth, and sometimes intense discussions. And you will be taking advantage of the very best educational experiences that community colleges have to offer.

8. Make Intellectual Connections among Courses

It may not count for a grade, but some of your best learning will take place when you take time to bring intellectual coherence to the wide range of courses you take each term and each year.

A growing number of community colleges are attempting to create opportunities for students to make the linkages among the seemingly disparate courses they take from the different disciplines, where they get only a sociological or biological or literary perspective. Learning communities and capstone courses (usually in the last year of college, courses that integrate, summarize, and synthesize prior coursework) are newer curricular efforts at many community colleges to bring the importance of cross-disciplinary perspectives to bear on particular issues and topics. If your college offers these innovative programs, you should take advantage of them. If these programs are not offered, you should still try to make these linkages.

The idea is simple enough. As scholars study the complex issues of their fields and of society, it makes sense that they would want to bring to bear the full power of the intellectual perspectives and understandings of thinkers from all disciplines and departments in higher education. The same would be true in your courses. However, our community colleges and universities are organized into departments according to their disciplines. Unfortunately, at many colleges, instructors from one department may not interact very frequently with their colleagues from the next department.

If you are studying environmental issues, you will need to know not only the science of the environment but also the social, political, economic, and humanistic understandings of the environment. If each of your courses focuses on just one discrete aspect of the environment, then it will be up to you to integrate the perspectives of all these fields as you attempt to better understand environmental issues. If you look at the environment only from the perspective of a biologist or an economist, you will be missing the full picture needed to make informed analyses.

If you intend to focus on the health sciences, the same is true. To better understand problems related to sexually transmitted diseases, for example, you will want to take a wide variety of courses in genetics and the sciences, education, economics, sociology, and literature, among others. However, you will also want to do the work of making connections among what you have learned in each of these courses. Without doing so, you may become an expert in one particular area of your field, but your expertise will be narrowly tailored and limited in its impact.

Make this one of your challenges in college. Know that you can be all of these—deep, broad, analytical, and able to connect the dots across disciplinary subject fields and course topics.

9. Become Skilled at Different Ways of Knowing

As a result of your many years of schooling and your life experiences, you have become an expert learner, or at least you are expert in some ways of learning. Community college offers you the opportunity to learn in many different ways. You would do well to explore these different paths to knowledge, to gain some experience with all of them, and to identify which approaches are best suited to your learning style.

Not everyone enjoys learning in the same way. Some of your peers find sheer joy in problem-solving math homework. Others love to spend hours in the science lab doing experiments and other hands-on work. One of our students described how, in third grade, when the other kids were playing ball at recess, she was busy writing, developing, and handing out questionnaires on all sorts of topics. What pathways to learning are most stimulating to you?

In community college, you will find yourself in smaller discussion classes as well as large lectures. There are benefits to both. Learn how to be an active participant in discussions and how to get the most out of listening to lectures.

In addition to these more traditional means, some students find that they love to learn through experiential approaches. Experiential learning might mean working in a local school as you study about education, children, or the life of cities. It could mean collecting and analyzing water samples as part of an environmental technology class or building automotive parts for new technologies as part of a workforce program. Critical to experiential learning is that you take time for study and reflection.

Other approaches might include discovery and exploration through a research paper, writing a thesis, collaborative or individual projects, and interdisciplinary study. You may have been encouraged or discouraged to develop your skills in certain methods and fields. Regardless of your previous experiences, you should strive to gain good skills in all these areas.

Finally, you should become serious about the learning opportunities you will find outside as well as inside the classroom. Attending lectures, readings, exhibits, and concerts, acting in a play, writing for the school newspaper, working as a peer mentor or in a department's office are all wonderfully rich learning opportunities that will provide you with skills, insights, and experiences that you cannot learn through lectures or books.

10. Schedule Time to Stay Involved in Campus Life to Learn Outside the Classroom

Some of the most important lessons learned in college take place outside the classroom.

You can learn from every individual you encounter and every activity you participate in, no matter where or when those interactions take place, as long as you make a point of reflecting on those encounters and experiences. Community college is an environment of intentional learning, and you should begin to think of yourself as an intentional learner. Maximize your opportunities for learning as deeply and as broadly as possible from all your college-related experiences.

If, like most community college students, you commute to campus and have a job to help pay your tuition, there are lots of reasons why it's more difficult for you to be actively involved in campus life, but none of those reasons are good enough to keep you away. You just have to make up your mind that you're going to be actively involved and then follow through on that commitment. It's important for your education, for your connections with professors and fellow students, and for your personal and social development. It will make a difference in the likelihood of your academic success.

One of the keys to both community college satisfaction and success is the degree to which you feel connected or linked to the institution. Feeling connected through academics is the best way to do this, but it's also critical to make these connections through campus-life activities. Even if you cannot join an organization, you should, if your schedule permits, plan on arriving early or staying on campus later one or two days each week. Try to leave some designated time in your campus schedule to attend events, especially ones that interest you personally or are directly connected to what you are studying in your courses.

Consider a variety of categories of learning outside the classroom. First, begin with what may seem to be the easiest and most natural, something like hanging out with friends. At college, you have a chance to broaden your scope of friends. Once you step on campus, you are likely to meet individuals who come from a much wider variety of orientation backgrounds than you have previously been exposed to or been friendly with. Students will be from different countries and from different parts of your own community. Their ethnic and religious backgrounds may be different from your own. Get to know these people. Make friends with them. In time, open up yourself to them about your background and learn about theirs.

Second, get involved in activities outside your courses. Join the newspaper, the choir, the chemistry club, an intramural sports team, or your student council. Volunteer for a community service project, or take on an internship. All of these activities will give you insight into how organizations and people within organizations work in different sectors of society. Are the organizations highly structured or unstructured, hierarchical or authority sharing? Do people involved work competitively or collaboratively, do they do things together outside of work, or does everyone go their own way immediately after a meeting or the job is done?

Third, attend all sorts of campus events, including those that are social, educational, and cultural. Attend a play, concert, comedian's performance, art exhibit, or poetry reading. Go to a debate about global warming, a presentation on race relations, a talk about the human genome, a workshop on balancing school, family, and work, or the opening of a movie made by independent filmmakers in your town. Go by yourself, with a friend, or with a large group from one of your classes. You will be exposed to a wide range of life from many different vantage points. Enjoy yourself, and learn about a different aspect of your community.

Fourth, get involved in campus and community organizations to learn leadership skills. Run for an office in student government. Train to become a tutor or a peer mentor. Be a site leader one day a week for the local food kitchen. Let a faculty member or dean know that you'd like to be a student representative on a college committee. Attend leadership workshops or retreats. You will learn about different kinds of leadership, where your strengths lie, and how you like to participate in organizations.

Finally, don't forget to take advantage of local theater performances, concerts, and museums, some of which you can attend at discounted student rates. Attending these may deepen the learning in your courses. It will certainly broaden your horizons immeasurably. If you haven't already, you should develop these habits for your entire life.

6

Expand Your Social Boundaries and Make a Difference in the World

1. Be Both a Thinker and an Activist: Take Responsibility for the World around You

Have you ever thought about what you would do if you had the power to make the world a better place? Whatever your age and background, community college is a time not just to think a lot about yourself—your professional and personal development, relationships, and academic success—but about how you can make a significant impact on the world around you. Just as there is a value in looking after our own well-being, we also need to look after the well-being of those around us.

Your attendance at community college places you among an elite group in the world. This is a privilege and opportunity you should not take lightly. It gives you rights and responsibilities that comparatively few people worldwide possess.

Make a commitment to yourself to be a thinking person who will make a difference in the world. Be a thoughtful agent for social change and social justice, regardless of your political perspective. Develop a passion for involvement and participation that is based on the analytical tools, complex thinking skills, and knowledge learned in your classes.

It's not enough to be just a good thinker or just an activist. You need to be both. You need to learn to apply your thoughtfulness into good practice.

Think for yourself. Listen to others' points of views, attend lectures, conferences, and information sessions, and read voraciously, but don't become just another ideologue. Your ability to think independently and to bring nuanced, critical reasoning to enormously complex problems is precisely what the world needs you to do with your college education. Don't go the simplistic, sound-bite, PR-managed route.

Don't assume there is only one right position or room for a debate between just two parties. There may be multiple truths to consider and multiple voices that need to be heard. Where it appears that no solution is to be found or that no one is standing up for what you believe, then take responsibility for finding that solution and standing up for yourself.

In college, you have an opportunity to investigate and better understand the historic and structural conditions that maintain inequalities and injustices within societies or across national borders. It may be frustrating, to some extent, to learn how difficult it is to find comprehensive solutions. However, your new knowledge and insights may empower you to take action to work for the changes necessary to bring about a more just society.

How do we take responsibility for the world around us? There's a whole range of approaches, and we all have to find the ways that best fit our personalities. One way to do this is through personal relationships: how you relate to acquaintances, friends, even strangers. Do you interrupt racist or homophobic jokes? Do you behave respectfully toward the person with whom you develop a romantic relationship? Do you speak openly and honestly about friends and family whether or not they are present?

If you are not already actively engaged in giving back to society, you might start now, by tutoring in a school, by volunteering in a hospital, or by serving in an organization and on its committees. Some take responsibility by running for political office, voting in elections, writing letters to the editor, or contesting the decisions of college administrators or political leaders.

Think about what good you want to do with your education. What can you do to make a change in the world, whether it be among your friends and family, in your community, your city, your state, or your nation or across national borders? Decide what approach best fits who you are. This process may take some time, but look at the world around you and decide how you can take advantage of the power and privilege that your community college education confers to make the world a more just place for everyone.

2. Do Community Service

Participating in a community service project is another way to expand your boundaries while you are in college. Some colleges offer formal community service projects for college credit; a few colleges even require them. At other colleges, instructors sometimes include community service projects as required or optional parts of their regular courses.

Making the time to get involved in community work during college is important for many reasons, particularly if you interact with members of a community with whom you are not familiar. First, you will learn a great deal about yourself as a result of meeting and interacting with people different from you. Those contacts will cause you to reflect on yourself, your family, your racial and class background, and the privileges and challenges that you have faced in your life. Second, you will learn an enormous amount about the community with which you work in terms of the people, their racial and economic backgrounds, and the meaning and challenges they find in their lives. Third, you will begin to become a deeper thinker by beginning to see things from the perspectives of people who view the world through a different lens.

These experiences are important, too, because you will be helping the community by making an important contribution. Most students don't realize just how important their impact is, whether it involves tutoring or mentoring children, visiting the elderly, or helping in an office. Community agencies depend on their volunteers' contributions, and while college students often think that what they do is inconsequential, children, seniors, and agency administrators all note the absence any time a volunteer doesn't show up when expected. It's important to realize that people depend on you and that you have a lot to offer.

You should recognize the distinction that community colleges make between community service and community service-learning. Many returning students already participate in church, school, or community organizations. High school students do community service out of a strong personal or ethical commitment, because it makes them feel good, in order to fulfill school requirements, or to build a good resume for college applications. What distinguishes these kinds of community service from service-learning is that service-learning requires you to read and reflect about your experience—it becomes part of your intellectual work at college in addition to service work.

What you will learn by reflecting on your service-learning project is, quite simply, the many types of service and the extent to which service and active participation in one's community are an important part of being a citizen in a strong democratic society.

You will also likely discover the wide variety of reasons people do community service, ranging from how good it sometimes feels to help others, to a sense of obligation for those with more privileges to help others who are less fortunate, to religious notions of charity. Some people do community service because they feel they are partners with people from all segments of society in creating a more just world for all. They may want to go beyond being charitable to making changes in the social structures of society that will help reduce the need for food kitchens and after-school tutors, and which will help create more jobs and better schools. These are the kinds of things you will want to reflect on in a service-learning project.

Another important lesson in service-learning is the deeper understanding you will gain about social issues and identities, including social justice and the content of the service project. As a student, you will have a chance to think more about your place in society and how that is affected by whether you are a member of a majority or minority social group. You will undoubtedly learn more about yourself as you learn more about the people you are serving in the community.

3. Don't Make Assumptions about People

You walk onto campus, and you see someone looking at you. You've never met this person, but you can tell that he or she is sizing you up. He or she is drawing a mental picture of who you are, putting you into a small and limiting box. The truth is that almost all of us do the same kind of sizing up of other people around us, drawing on stereotypical images to make judgments about the unique individuals around us.

So what's the problem? The problem is that when others do this to us or we do the same to others around us, we lose sight of the very special, unique characteristics that each of us prides ourselves on as individuals. We erase the individuality and soul of each person around us. And, as is usually the case, we miss out on opportunities to meet all kinds of amazing people.

The stereotyping and dismissal of people based on physical characteristics represents a tremendous opportunity lost, especially for college students. Yet in college, many students are inclined to go ahead and forge friendships with or avoid people based on grand assumptions based on so little (mis)information. Some of us will set high or low expectations of people based on what region of the country they come from. We might have preconceived ideas about people from New York or Texas. Yet, surely, if we paused for just an instant, all of us would know that any one person cannot possibly be exactly like the other millions of people in a city like New York City or state like Texas.

The sad part is that far too many of your fellow students may be judging you in the same way. How wrong and simplistic can they be? Yet all these college students are supposed to be so smart!

Our hope is that you will be just a little bit smarter than they are. Try this: Every time you meet a new person, withhold your assumptions about him or her. Try to actually meet and get to know the person behind the handbag, the t-shirt, the skin color, the home town, the accent, or the age, weight, and height. Get to know each person's individual values, history, aspirations, humor, and friends. Find out about others just as you'd hope they would want to learn about you.

We think this approach not only will give you a chance to make real, lasting friendships with people from all backgrounds but along the way will help you to learn to like yourself a lot more as you give yourself and others a chance to grow beyond the little boxes into which we paint ourselves.

4. Participate Actively in Civic Life

An engaged citizenry makes for a strong society by discussing ideas, sharing news, engaging in public life, and building community.

You may already be involved in your community. However, if you haven't had the time or haven't thought about this before, here are a number of ways you can learn how your community college education is as much about your community and your role in strengthening it as it is about the other aspects of your life.

One of the great strengths of community colleges is that they are, often quite literally, their "community's" college. You may be enrolled at one of the colleges in the country that takes this mission seriously and offers courses that focus on issues that are relevant to the surrounding community or region. What are the issues that matter in your community or state? What knowledge and skills are needed to help address those? Are there courses that could help you become informed and able to contribute to solutions? Consider taking those courses.

What are the political concerns in your community? Who votes in local and national elections? Who does not vote? Do you vote? When only a few people vote, it means that a small elite is getting to make the decisions for you about who runs our cities, our states, and our country. That's not very democratic. Attend a city council meeting, and voice your opinion. Go to your town's school board meetings. Write a letter to the editor of your newspaper. Fewer and fewer citizens are involved in local politics. Again, that means that a small minority are making decisions about how we should live our lives.

Your community college is also itself a community. What are the issues on your campus? Who is involved in student government? Who makes decisions about matters that affect students? Consider running for a student government office. If you cannot, learn about who is running. Ask them questions. Talk with other students and faculty and staff. Vote.

Make the concerns of your neighborhood and surrounding towns and cities and your campus your business. Yes, it does take all of us to keep the nation's democracy healthy and vibrant for this generation and those to follow. If we don't care about the people in our community, state, and nation, we can't expect that elected officials will care about you or your neighbors. Citizens in a democratic nation look after other citizens and take responsibility for the good of the whole.

Most important of all, get a good education. Democracies need educated citizens—citizens and leaders who can think critically, reason analytically, and size up complex problems from many different perspectives. An uneducated, uninformed citizenry is more likely to follow demagogues and fail to challenge bad ideas from wrongheaded leaders. People like you, who will be well educated and involved in society, are our nation's best hope for a strong, diverse democracy.

5. Develop Effective Leadership Skills

One of the goals of higher education is to develop an informed citizenry who will be active participants and leaders in a diverse world. You want to emerge from your community college education as one of those active participants and leaders.

There are many different types of leaders and many different leadership opportunities. You should consider trying all of them to acquire experience and skills but also to see what fits you best. You have probably already had experience with the traditional model of leadership—a single head of a hierarchically arranged organization. But there are other kinds of leadership.

In your classes, you can be an intellectual leader. You do this when you come to class not only prepared (having completed the assignment) but also ready to ask probing questions and offer critical insights about the day's assignments. You also are an intellectual leader when you are a good listener and respond appropriately to other students' comments. As a leader, you can help organize study groups and support your fellow students who raise good issues or who come to you with questions.

Leaders help resolve conflicts. At work or in an apartment you share with others, you will be confronted with occasional conflicts, arguments over procedures, inconsiderate and rude behavior, and perhaps even racial or religious insensitivities. These situations require someone who emerges as a leader, someone who will set a positive tone and create an environment in which people learn to talk through differences and disagreements.

Some people act as leaders through their ability to collaborate effectively with others. Working effectively in teams is a skill that most people require in all aspects of life, from the office to the community to home. Yet it is an exceedingly difficult skill and one that few people fully master. Finding opportunities to develop this skill through study groups, group papers, lab projects, and planning events for student organizations will serve you well and give you valuable experience.

Another way to learn effective collaboration is to purposefully engage in meaningful ways with people and settings that are new to you. Sadly, even in college, students encounter walls that divide people and organizations. By intentionally working to expand your comfort zone, you can gain a level of ease being with people from different social backgrounds. By getting to know the persons behind particular viewpoints, you will discover how even well-educated, well-meaning, and very likeable people can differ dramatically on politics and issues of intellectual interest. By taking a broad array of courses across various disciplines, you will gain an understanding about why and how different people can be so intrigued by and even passionate about topics that you hadn't even heard of. With these experiences you can be the one to find common ground and opportunity in difference.

Leadership can also mean finding your voice and taking a stand. There are many competing news items about social issues and loads of sound-bite answers to complex questions that truly require clear, critical, and complex answers. As a college-educated person, you can demonstrate the importance of understanding issues and arriving at answers that go beyond traditional, simplistic solutions. You can do this with national and global issues but also with issues on campus: Is tuition too high? Should the library be open on weekends? Should carpools get reserved parking?

Finally, in addition to all of these informal opportunities to develop leadership skills, many community colleges offer formal opportunities. Your might have an opportunity to demonstrate leadership by serving as a student assistant or facilitator of course discussions as a peer mentor and in other situations. Taking on a role like this requires responsibility, organizational skills, good discussion and listening skills, and the ability to assert oneself and intervene when necessary. Student government associations, advisory councils, and program boards provide great opportunities for developing leadership abilities. Many community colleges also offer classes, workshops, and retreats on leadership. In these activities, you will do readings, review case studies, and learn what makes good leaders in all of the different situations where leadership exists and is necessary.

6. Model a Sustainable Lifestyle

How are we going to survive as a planet? What responsibility, if any, do you have while at your college for helping ensure that we use resources wisely and sustainably?

You don't have to be an environmentalist to understand that your choices have an impact on your life today as well as the lives of future generations and that careful use of resources provides you and your community and college with a variety of benefits. Whatever political stance you hold about national and global policies, you should examine how your decisions and your behavior affect your local community and even national and global communities.

Many community colleges have begun to make conscious efforts to evaluate how the college's practices affect the surrounding community. Some of this effort takes place in the classroom as faculty and students analyze the economic, health, and political consequences of transportation, water use, waste production, sustainable agriculture, and the impact of increasing globalization of local communities.

It is important, however, that this understanding not just stay in the classroom. What are the local initiatives at your community college and in your community to transition toward more sustainable practices? Is there public transportation to get around? Does the college provide incentives for students to carpool to campus? Does the college cafeteria purchase locally grown food? What policy initiatives can your campus and town undertake to create a more sustainable present and future for all of us?

For that matter, do you drive, walk, or ride a bike? Because, of course, you will want to consider your own role in these matters. Have you considered the extent to which you are a consumer of the world's resources? Have you evaluated your use of electricity, technology, water, and fuel? What are your recycling habits? Do you know the size of your carbon footprint? What about your own food choices? How can you contribute to the sustainability of our resources and the planet's health for generations to come?

You might be tempted to think that these are matters to take up later, after you finish your college education. But now, while you are in college, is exactly the time to learn about these issues and how they affect you, your career, your family, and your community.

7. Engage in Dialogue with People Who Are Different from You

Imagine this experience in your community college: white students in a small class talking with students of color; gay students in conversation with straight students; men and women talking honestly together; anti-war students talking to military veterans; students meeting with their peers from different religious backgrounds or who have different first languages; U.S.-born students conversing with students who have immigrated from other countries; U.S. students engaged in activities with international students. You could be participating in these intergroup dialogues.

Across the country, more and more high schools and colleges are establishing courses or programs to help students engage in in-depth, serious conversations with fellow students from different social backgrounds.

It's sometimes hard for many students like you to find a safe space to ask one another the really hard questions about race, gender, sexual orientation, religious difference, and so on. It's very possible that many of you have never had the experience of a deep and sustained conversation with others about the important and enduring issues of difference, commonalities, equalities, and inequalities based on our social identities.

Most students, like you, are very eager for these conversations, yet we all know how hard it is to speak openly about our society's long-standing divisions and conflicts. Intergroup dialogues can be organized through courses or programs. These are structured to give you and other students a chance to meet one another as individuals and as members of various social identity groups, develop a degree of trust in the dialogue group, and build a safe space in which to engage the truly difficult issues that so often divide us. If your community college doesn't offer formal intergroup dialogue classes, look for conversation partners, retreats, even courses like intercultural communication that are often organized around these practices.

Students talk about intergroup dialogues as being transformative experiences. What is so exciting about them is that they give you a chance to open the doors to the potential of a diverse society by participating in an updated version of the nineteenth-century New England town hall meeting, where citizens took active control and responsibility for the life of the community and the democratic society. Instead of being held back by the fear and invisible walls that keep people apart, students who participate in dialogues are able to personally engage with their peers on campus and embrace a world that brings all people together.

Finally, you are more likely to find that the professional world that awaits you when you graduate will be looking for someone just like you, a person who can work effectively with people from all different backgrounds as employees, co-workers, and supervisors.

8. Learn a Second (or Third) Language

Many of today's community college students speak English as their second, third, or fourth language. However, many others only speak English and have never taken a class to learn another language. Like many U.S. citizens, they may wonder why there is even a need for language instruction in another language. After all, English is spoken throughout the United States and in many parts of the world. If this describes you, stop wondering, and start studying another language.

The world grows smaller and more interconnected each day. For you, as today's community college student and tomorrow's professional, the nations of the world will seem much more like the proverbial global village than anyone can begin to imagine now. Further, the multilingual global village increasingly resides not just in foreign countries but within the U.S. borders as well.

The speed of travel, the instant communication of the global Internet, the rapid expansion of global business networks, and the natural resources that know no boundaries and that we increasingly share across the globe will lead us to have much more frequent and consistent contact with people everywhere. Literature, movies, politics, business, and trade cross our borders every day whether or not we choose to acknowledge the massive interdependence of the peoples throughout the world.

It has always been the case, and it is no different today, that we know we can understand and communicate better across cultures if we know the language of different cultures. Language in translation is considerably different and less rich than the original. The precise meanings, the cultural understandings, and the delicate nuances of language cannot be adequately captured in translation.

Much of the world already speaks more than one language. As you increasingly think of yourself as a global citizen as well as a citizen of a particular nation, you might need to speak more than one language to keep up. Even the United States is increasingly becoming a bilingual or multilingual nation, and to move comfortably across the business and cultural sectors within this society, you should be conversant in more than one language.

When you apply for a job or a promotion, you will not want to be held back because you can't speak the language of your customers and clients. When you watch a movie, you will not want to be relegated to reading subtitles. When you read newspapers online from many different nations, you will want to read the original text. When you meet friends and colleagues from different backgrounds, you will want to freely converse and communicate deeply with them in both your and their first languages. And when you travel abroad, you will want to speak that country's language.

PART 4

SUCCESSFUL CHOICES FOR YOUR LIFE AND CAREER

7

Explore Your Relationships, Choices, Identity, and Inner Self

1. Explore, Affirm, and Own Your Life Choices

One of the most exciting opportunities of adulthood is identifying who we are and making our own choices. This is an ongoing process that starts when we are very young and continues throughout our lives. For many young people, community college is one of the first opportunities to make choices solely on their own, without parents and other adults setting the parameters. For others, who return to college after a few or many years away from school, being in college can be an opportunity to reevaluate choices and set the stage for a different future.

To evaluate your choices, you will need to step back and see all the old things you've been doing in your life with new eyes and perspectives. And you should remain open to trying new things and examine the effect of those as well. It takes both experience and reflection to be able to judge the short-term and long-term impact of your choices.

Your choices come in many shapes and forms, big and small, significant and less significant. Most important, however, you also get to choose your classes and your major. Many people will advise you and tell you what you should study. Listen carefully to what they say because they mean well, have a lifetime of experience to share with you, and can serve as important resources and support for you. And of course you will need to pay attention to the requirements imposed by your community college. If you are receiving financial aid or support for vocational rehabilitation, you will need to pay attention to requirements set by these programs as well.

But even with such limits, you are the one who must choose selections that make sense to you. Sometimes students come to us concerned because a family member—a parent or partner—is opposed to their choice of major or career. Our questions are always the same: What are your reasons for your choice? Have you thought through the consequences of choosing this major or career? And our advice is always this: whether your choice leads to the career you desire or to other results, you are the one who must live with your choice. In five years or ten years, when you wake up in the morning, you want to be able to say that, whatever has happened, you made the best choice for you.

The knowledge that you are in charge of your choices can be both thrilling and frightening. That's how freedom is. That's what life is about. When you break the rules, they are your rules. And when you set forth on your own path, it's your path and choices, your accomplishments and failures, and the meaning and fulfillment are your own.

Community college offers you a chance to reaffirm the choices you've been making in your life or to put those aside and try out some new ones. If you do this right, it will be a continual process that lasts throughout your lifetime. Give yourself time and space to do this. Most of all, give yourself the power to shape your own life.

2. Reexamine Your Values ‒‒‒

Who am I? What matters most to me? And, what does that have to do with my being here at this community college?

The weight of important existential questions of life can feel like a heavy burden particularly in the middle of huge transitions— changing your career, being part of a new culture, shifting from high school to college or from military to civilian life. But these questions are essential for moving forward in life. Particularly if you have never done so before, it is critical that you start the process of questioning while you are in college.

We often ask first-year students to write essays about their individual and group identities or their experiences and goals. Students embrace this assignment because it allows them to look back on their experiences and reflect on their values, their ideals, and their identities. They write outstanding papers for this assignment, and we encourage you to do the same. But, invariably, they will ask how anyone can possibly grade them on their identity. We tell them that we value each one of our students as an A person, an extraordinary individual, with a unique and exceptional life story. But we grade the essay, not the person. It is the ability of each student to tell his or her story in the most thoughtful and reflective manner that will determine the grade.

That's what we would say to you, too. During college, you should begin in earnest to shape and tell the story of what you find when you look deeply inside to discover who you are now, what you value most, and who you want to be and what you hope to accomplish in your lifetime. The deeper you allow yourself to probe and explore, the better able you will be to move forward with a strong foundation. Don't be concerned if the answers aren't easily or immediately found. This is a process that should and does take time.

This process of introspection almost without exception begins to take place in earnest during periods of dramatic change, so it's best for you to take control of it now. You will find yourself with a whole new set of people surrounding you, new classmates, new teachers, new friends. With these new people and surroundings, you have a unique opportunity to explore, experiment, establish, and assert your identity and who you want to be in life.

Whether your time in college is unstructured or jammed with responsibilities, taking the time to reflect on your purpose in life, your values, and your identity is an invaluable part of learning.

3. Take Care of Your Inner-Self

As much as your intellect and your physical body need your care, attention, and stimulation, so does your inner life. While you may feel that juggling work, school, and family is enough responsibility to keep in mind, you should remember that caring for yourself is important to help you be strong enough to face each day.

Beyond any material goals or even academic achievements, what is important to you in life? What are your values? When you get down to the essentials in your life, what matters most? What keeps you going each day? What is your purpose in life?

If you are having academic troubles in your classes, you will know from your grades or because your professor will speak to you. If you are stimulated by your teachers and by the related intellectual content of the courses, your mind will let you know. When you are healthy or not feeling well or have sustained an injury, your body will tell you.

It's just as important to have some mechanisms to keep track of whether your soul is healthy or aching. Do people speak well of you, the person, not just of your accomplishments or the clothes you wear? Do your friends like you because of your generous spirit, or do they like you because you own a car or have access to the latest technologies? Do you like yourself because of your good looks, because of awards you have received, or because you like what you stand for in the world?

Do you feel good about who you are? Do you not only like the personality you present to others but also like the person inside whom you know better than anyone else? Can you not only live with yourself but also appreciate and respect who you are?

You may want to determine what nurtures your inner self. It might be a good friendship. It might be good family relationships. You could be heartened by the story of someone's life that you read about in a book or watch in a movie. Perhaps you feel good after doing something nice for another person, for your community, or for an animal or for the environment. You might need to learn something new and inspiring, appreciate a work of art or music, or gain insight into something you never understood before. Your soul might be nurtured by your connection with your faith or god or by appreciating the bounty of the earth when you eat some fresh fruit and vegetables. You might get this feeling from a deeply moving conversation with a friend, a teacher, a parent, or grandparent or from the joy of holding a newborn baby.

Being healthy has many dimensions. Be sure you take care of your body and mind, but be just as concerned with your essence, your inner self.

4. Embrace Change as You Examine Your Social Roles and Personal Choices

Major life changes of any kind affect every aspect of our lives. This is true whether the changes are positive or negative. And it is true whether the changes come from our choices or events over which we have no control. Whatever led to your decision to attend community college, you will likely find yourself experiencing some of the emotions that accompany major transitions—excitement, anxiety, and perhaps even doubt about yourself and your choices. This should not be a cause for alarm. Instead, it presents you with the opportunity to explore who you are and who you would like to become.

As part of exploring your identity you will want to examine all the different roles you play in your life. Which ones are most important to you and which are not? Is there balance in your different roles or are you tied very closely to just one? How do you fulfill your different roles? Are there parts that are deeply satisfying for you and parts that you would like to change? How do you perceive yourself, your character, behavior, and values? Are there patterns in your life that you would like to change? How confident are you with the choices you make for yourself?

Some people are not aware of the extent to which they identify themselves with a particular role or pursuit—for instance, parent, soldier, welder, doctor, or mountain climber—until that role changes. Most of us have heard of older people who have defined themselves so strongly by their careers that they cannot adjust to retirement or parents who cannot stop parenting once their children are grown. You may not realize that enrolling in community college can create similar feelings. If you are just out of high school, you may find yourself overwhelmed by the transition to adulthood and taking responsibility for yourself. In contrast, if you are returning to college after being away from school for a while, you may find yourself struggling with the shift from thinking of yourself as a competent and successful adult to thinking of yourself as a "student."

In college, the opportunity to explore frequently develops when you least expect it. You may have convinced yourself that you have never been good at math but find yourself enjoying math and even contemplating a math major. You may have always loved writing but suddenly find yourself struggling to write the kind of papers required for your program. You may have always wanted to become an engineer only to discover that you have a great talent for poetry. These are important discoveries, ones you should examine very carefully.

You can also create the opportunities to explore your roles and sense of self. If you feel conflicted about working on a paper instead of spending time with your children, you have an opportunity to redefine how you parent. If you have always been a follower, take the lead on a group project as a way to explore your own leadership potential. If you are a perfectionist who shoulders most of the work in groups, step back and be willing to accept "good enough" on that project or be pleasantly surprised at the high quality of your fellow group members' work. This will not only help you, but it can create opportunities for other members of your group to share the workload and responsibility.

Whatever your community college experience, remind yourself often that you are in a period of transition. Remind yourself that your identity is comprised of many different roles and that these roles change—and should change—over time. Be patient with yourself and with these changes.

5. Investigate Your Social Identities

In addition to the personal identity that you have developed based on your personal values and choices, you also have social identities. This means that your personal identity is linked to the social identity of many other people. These social identities include ethnic identity, racial identity, religious identity, economic class identity, gender identity, sexual orientation identity, and so forth. For many of you, your social identity includes more than one group within each of these categories, such as more than one ethnic, racial, or religious identity.

Social identities are very significant in our lives. You may choose—or not choose—to embrace the values, histories, cultures, traditions, and other beliefs and practices associated with a group that is part of your social identity. However, people and institutions outside the group will typically hold attitudes and act in certain ways toward you simply on the basis of your social identity, regardless of your degree of commitment to the group.

Social identities matter. The history of our civilization and of this country tells repeated stories of oppression and injustices toward people based solely on their social identities. Even though all students at your community college have in common the fact that they are attending the same college and taking similar classes, there may be strong pressures to try to limit the kinds of people with whom you become friends and associate based solely on their social identities. We all have made assumptions and often acted in particular ways toward other individuals based strictly on their race, gender, religion, and economic class.

At the same time, if you are clear and thoughtful about the social disadvantages and privileges that are based on your various social identities, you may have the courage and conviction to challenge some of these barriers. In so doing, you will find that you are able to both explore a much broader set of friendships than you had while growing up and help to establish a world based on social justice for people from all backgrounds.

6. Take Time to Nurture Relationships with Your Family

Since so many community college students are the first in their families to attend college, many do not understand that the decision to go to college disrupts old routines and rearranges priorities. This is true not just for you, the student, but for your family as well. Some families adjust quickly to these changes, but others do not. Whether you are living at home with parent(s) or your spouse or your partner and/or children or have moved away for the first time, you will likely notice changes in your relationships with your family when you attend community college.

The choice to go to college often reshapes expectations and roles for couples. You may find you have less time or energy to do what you used to do for your family or with them. If your partner has taken a job to provide financial support for you to go to school or has assumed greater responsibility for the household or children, you may find that the changes are even more dramatic. Even when families are supportive of your decision to attend college, it takes time to adjust to new rhythms and responsibilities. Your family may not understand why you are not as available as you used to be to make cookies or serve as the coach for your daughter's soccer team. They may be resentful or hurt if they feel that your studies seem more important to you than their needs or desires.

If you are young and living away from home for the first time, your parents may have difficulty adjusting to thinking of you as an adult rather than someone who needs their constant guidance. However, college is a time when you can and should refashion your relationship with others as an adult. Of course, this means you must take responsibility for your decisions about studying, taking courses, managing your finances, paying your taxes, etc. You will always be the child of your parent(s), but you should begin the transition from being just the child to being an independent adult in relationship with your parent(s).

You will want to make sure that you take time to nurture these relationships and work with your loved ones as you all adjust to your new circumstances. Your family is one of your greatest resources for advice, for comfort on a bad day, and of course for praise for your grades or a major project you have completed. Transitions do not happen overnight, but if you take time and work at it, your relationships will thrive and, in many ways, become more meaning-ful. Most faculty and staff at community colleges will tell you that their favorite experience of the year is seeing and hearing families come to celebrate the graduation of their mothers, fathers, spouses, and partners as well as their sons and daughters. In the long run, you and your family will happily look forward to an ever deeper and more loving relationship in the many decades that lie ahead.

7. Analyze Your Successes and Failures

Sometimes students lament, "I can't understand why I didn't do well on that test. I studied harder than ever." Some students, particularly in their first term in college, may work especially hard on their studies and still not earn a passing grade. It's really frustrating to spend hours doing homework and preparing for class and tests but not achieve the results you had hoped for. That's why simply increasing the hours that you spend on every class may not be the best approach for learning. Instead, recognize that it takes times to make the transition to college, be patient with yourself, and, most important, analyze how you are studying for each course.

It can't be said enough: there are certain general principles for studying effectively that work for most people. You should always study when you are most alert, preferably early in the day. Delaying studying until the end of your work day or school day, when you may be tired, likely means you will spend more time with less effect. Study in a non-distracting environment. Distractions can sometimes double or triple your study time and reduce its effectiveness. Start with the most challenging assignment so that you are at your intellectual best for the hardest work. You know best what will provide you with a good break, one that refreshes you for returning to your studies rather than distracting you for long periods or permanently.

In addition, however, look very carefully at your own learning style and try to match that with what and how you are studying. If you are a visual learner, you may struggle to take a test on materials that you have heard only once in a lecture. If your classmates are good at learning from what they hear, they may do well on a test about a lecture but not as well as you do responding to a written passage. Your instructors are probably not going to tailor their classes and evaluations for your particular learning style. You can, however, tailor your approach to learning so that you build on your strengths.

The issue of learning styles is particularly important when it comes to online classes. Before you take any, make sure that you are fully prepared for the differences. Obviously, of course, you need to be able to use the technology used for your college's courses, including test taking, submitting work, and communicating with the instructor and student groups. Instead of listening to lectures and asking questions, your primary interactions will be through reading the course materials, textbook, and discussion threads. So it is important to consider that in exchange for flexibility in your schedules, online courses require enormous self-discipline, motivation, good reading and communication skills, and a great deal of your time.

Finally, you may also need to adapt your approach to learning for different community college courses. If your assignments require that you apply what you are learning in new contexts, then just memorizing vocabulary will not lead to success. The creative writing style that works for your assignment in a theater class probably won't receive good marks in a social problems class. And when it comes to tests, you should match how you study with how your learning will be evaluated. If your exams require short essay answers, then practice writing out short essay answers. If tests and quizzes are timed, then practice timing yourself.

A student in one of our classes was sure she would never pass math. Although she studied long and hard and always felt she understood the material, she was disappointed by her test scores. When she examined her math study patterns, she discovered a mismatch between how she studied and how she was tested. Every night she did her homework problems in an online math lab. For tests, however, she had to write out problems by hand and show her work. Once she began to copy out all of the online math homework and solve each problem in writing before entering her answer on the computer, she began to receive A's on her math tests.

There are so many different learners and so many different kinds of courses in community college that there is no single formula that works best for everyone. However, if you spend a bit of time analyzing your strengths and your situation, you can develop strategies that will help you make the best use of your own time.

8. Let Go of the Small Stuff

Perhaps you are one of those students who hold unbelievably high standards of success for yourself. Perhaps you have always done well in school while working a part-time job. Or you have always been an exemplary worker and cherished your family life. Why should enrolling in college change that? In fact, perhaps you plan to maintain your high standards in every aspect of your life. Although you have enrolled full time in college, you may decide to continue working full time and maintaining a great social life. If you are a parent, you might decide to continue as pack leader for your son's scout troop and host your entire extended family at your home for the holidays. Why shouldn't you be able to do it all?

Students who are returning to community college after time away are especially susceptible to this kind of thinking. You are ambitious and eager to reach your goals. And you will. But if you are not careful, you can burn out too quickly.

The real secret to success is to recognize that you can neither do all nor be all to everyone at all times. No one can. For most of your life you have been making choices about what is important to you, whether your choices were made on the spur of the moment or as part of a plan. Now that you are enrolled in community college, however, you need to consider your choices in terms of your long-term goals. You can let other parents volunteer at the grammar school while you are enrolled in college. Missing one or two nights out with your friends won't end your relationship. It's OK to cut back a bit on the household chores while you are finishing your research paper. And you will definitely want to find ways to have enough energy to finish each term successfully, even if it means establishing new holiday traditions.

If you haven't yet, you should list the long-range goals you established. Post them somewhere visible. When you get caught up in the busy details of each day, that list will remind you that you can't meet your goals unless you have clear priorities. Day by day, with each decision, make progress toward your goals. And as you do, you will find it is a great relief to let go of the small stuff.

8

Be Healthy, Safe, and Smart in Mind and Body

1. Live a Balanced Life

Balance is a core principal for having a successful community college experience. To take the best advantage of what community college can offer, you need to find ways to be a well-rounded person who takes advantage of the wide range of available opportunities.

Your challenge during college is to succeed academically but at the same time to allow yourself to thrive in all aspects of your life. Many students think of their time in community college as different from the rest of their lives because of the need to rearrange priorities for academic success. You might be tempted to focus only on studies, take too many credits, or schedule every waking moment, but you want to practice a healthy, balanced lifestyle that you can sustain throughout your life. To do this, you will need to learn to effectively manage your time and make difficult choices.

If college is your only focus and you have a lot of unstructured time, you may find yourself staying up late but wondering where all the hours of the day went. You will be thrilled with all the wonderful opportunities to learn and participate outside the classroom, but in order to keep your head in the books, you'll have to learn to say no sometimes to those activities and even to family and good friends.

If you are juggling work, family, and school, the opposite may be the case. You'll have to learn to say yes, to go out, be with friends and family, and do things outside of the classroom and work to make space to relax and enjoy all aspects of your life. The stress and intensity in college are very real, and it's important to get away from your studies, now and then.

Some students think they can succeed if they study hard and party hard. But be careful about establishing patterns that can lead to extremes, like workaholic or alcoholic tendencies. We advocate lightening up a bit on yourself and developing a balanced and well-rounded lifestyle that you can sustain over your lifetime. Learn to enjoy your studies, enjoy learning, enjoy your time with friends, and love life itself.

2. Sleep, Eat, and Exercise ━━━

While in college, some students get so busy that they push their bodies to their limit and beyond—and, as a result, they become ill, sometimes quite seriously. Even students who return to school after time away are surprised to discover that they too can become vulnerable to illness. They admit that they haven't followed the advice they give their own children: get plenty of sleep, eat well, exercise regularly, and wash your hands often. If you follow this advice, you will be healthy enough to enjoy college and withstand the stressful times. Ignore your body, and even if you don't become ill, you will be sluggish and won't be able to participate at 100 percent to do everything you want at college, at home, and at work.

Don't forget to sleep. The truth is that too many students—both young and old—get too little sleep on a regular basis and more than a few skip sleeping entirely. While it's true that some students start to study well after things quiet down in the wee hours of the morning, most students' academic productivity and retention decreases dramatically once they get tired. You will need to discover which times you are most alert and able to concentrate on your studies— whether it is after or before work or when your children are asleep or doing their homework.

All-nighters are not a good idea generally. The work in college is difficult, complex, and challenging, even when you are alert. Most people's attention spans and ability to focus decrease rapidly as they get tired. Rather than studying ahead of time, some students resort to drinking cup after cup of coffee or other caffeine stimulants or to taking speed or over-the-counter medications to keep themselves awake throughout the night. The results can be pretty ugly the day after, especially if the caffeine withdrawal hits during the exam or test. More important, the fact that you are resorting to stimulants for the sake of writing a paper or studying for an exam should serve as a wake-up call to you. It's just not a winning strategy for long-term success.

Eating may also present new challenges. Some students reward themselves by snacking or think they are saving time by relying on fast foods. Others get so involved with assignments or a major campus activity that they skip meals, thinking they will grab something later. But if you eat poorly or miss meals, you'll feel weaker, be more stressed, have less internal stamina to constructively manage all the activities in your life, and be more vulnerable to getting sick.

Regular exercise is equally important, not just for your physical health but for your mental health as well. You may need to adopt new routines or find new ways to get your body moving, but be sure to keep active. You can run alone or with others, play sports, or work out in a gym. If you do not already belong to a gym or cannot afford a membership, check out your community college facilities. Some campuses have recreational facilities, including all manner of strength and exercise machines, tracks, and courts for basketball. Some offer exercise classes from yoga to the latest strength training regimens.

While you may at times be tempted to skip a workout, don't. Take walks or a yoga class. Go to the gym. By exercising your body, you will feel renewed, and you will find that your mind is refreshed as well. You will come back from exercise with some new and probably more constructive insights about conflicts you are facing, problems you need to solve, studying you need to do, and tasks you need to accomplish. It will help to reduce the clutter in your mind and allow you to move more happily and productively through your day.

Silly as it may sound, don't forget to dress appropriately for the weather. Don't worry first about fashion. Use an umbrella. Bring a raincoat, warm clothing, and some good boots with you in case the weather changes. It's more fashionable to be healthy and participating in everything than to stay in bed with a fever.

What about when you're starting to feel a little under the weather? Again, listen to your body. If your throat is sore, drink some hot tea or orange juice and eat a bowl of chicken soup. If you're more tired than usual, get extra sleep.

You already know all this advice. Practice it, even while in college, and your body will thank you by working at full efficiency.

3. Be Safe in Sex

You may have already had this thought: I know about safe sex; I don't need to keep reading. But it is quite remarkable how uninformed people are about the consequences of sexual activity. Some obvious consequences, of course, are unplanned pregnancies and, possibly, difficult personal choices about abortion or raising a child. But are you aware that there are a great many different kinds of STDs (Sexually Transmitted Diseases) and STIs (Sexually Transmitted Infections), and that many are asymptomatic—that is, a person can be unknowingly infected (and can infect others), sometimes for years, without experiencing symptoms?

Sexual choices are serious ones, with personal, emotional, social, religious, and health ramifications. Whether you're a man or a woman, straight or gay, young or older, you need to become educated about safe sex. If you don't know how to protect yourself and your prospective partner, take time to get a crash course on the subject. You and your partner's health and life depend on it.

An important first step is to be thoughtful and conscientious about the choice to be sexually active. Before starting a new sexual relationship, both you and your partner will want to be tested for the most common STDs.

And of course, one of the best ways that sexually active people can avoid having unsafe sex is to remain sober. The likelihood of having unwanted and unprotected sex rises exponentially if you are under the influence of alcohol or other drugs.

Another way that sexually active people can avoid unprotected sex is to talk with their partners about safe sex. Too many students are too skittish to talk about sexual relations and sex education, even though they've been exposed to TV shows, Internet, and movies that seem totally consumed with sex. Be sure that you talk and that you are both committed to using protection and being safe every time you engage in sexual activity.

Talk to a doctor, nurse, peer health educator, or staff at the health center to learn how to protect yourself. Create an informal support network of friends, female and male alike, to make sure everyone in your group is well educated and has all the protective devices available. One of our students, a football player, did community service with an organization responsible for educational outreach about HIV/AIDS. During his training and subsequent outreach work, his awareness and concern about safe sex increased dramatically. One day he came to office hours to explain that he realized that many of his teammates were putting themselves and their partners in jeopardy because they were so poorly educated about safe sex and because so little protection was being used. He said that he had begun distributing condoms to the football team and asking around to see if there was interest in more education.

Follow this student's lead. Get educated. Get condoms and other protection for safe sex. Think about these issues now, well before you find yourself in a situation when it will be much harder to start the discussion. Find friends who care enough about you and each other to support one another to always be protected and prepared. This is everyone's responsibility: yours, your partner's, and your friends—men and women alike.

4. Make Smart, Informed, and Lawful Choices about Alcohol and Other Substances

If you are living on your own for the first time, you will be able to do pretty much whatever you choose with regard to alcohol and drugs. It is, therefore, important that you give some thought to your use of alcohol and other substances so you make a smart, informed, and lawful choice.

You probably won't be able to avoid this question. Alcohol and drugs will be widely available, and there will be both friendly encouragement and sometimes pressure from friends and social groups to drink and use drugs. Students you know and like will invite you to drink, smoke marijuana, or try other drugs, and these will be available at many parties. You may also be encouraged to buy and use prescription drugs to stay alert for your studies.

This widespread use and availability has some serious consequences. The yearly results of data gathered on drinking, binge drinking (excessive alcohol consumption in a short period of time), and abuse of prescription and other drugs shows that the rate of use by college students is increasing.

Come to college having given some thought about how you want to act. You will need to have enough confidence in yourself to be able to act on your own choices. If it is your choice, you need to be able to say no when an offer presents itself. You also need confidence to be able to say yes initially, but also no later, before you've had too much.

One key issue to think about is why you want to drink or use drugs. Perhaps you can't feel relaxed or sociable without a few drinks. Maybe you think your life is too boring and humdrum and that you can't experience the highs of life that others seem to have without getting high. Perhaps you are convinced that you can't maintain your concentration or stamina for your studies or sports without using drugs. In any of these situations, you will want to examine your own beliefs and attitudes about yourself and weigh the short-term gains—confidence, fun, and performance—against the long-term impact.

Your use of alcohol and other drugs in college is ultimately a decision about your mental, emotional, and physical health. Understanding why, whether, and how much you choose to use alcohol or drugs will help you discover more about the life you lead, about the degree of happiness and fulfillment in your life, and what changes you might want to consider making about your very essence. These are important decisions. Choose wisely.

5. Take Precautions for Your Personal Safety

Most community colleges, even those campuses in areas with higher crime rates, have a feeling of safety. Community colleges tend to be supportive, safe environments, with teachers, counselors, peer advisors, and friends all looking out for you. You can easily get the feeling that the worst that could befall you is a bad grade on a test or that a bureaucratic person in the registrar's office won't give you the course you want.

Sadly, however, even community college students can be victims of crimes of opportunity. You should take some simple, common-sense precautions to prevent thefts and ensure your personal safety.

Thieves often target college areas. Some have figured out that they can sit at the entrance to large campus parking lots and watch for cars with great sound systems and other electronics that are easy to grab. They wait until students have raced to class and then quickly break in and take what they want. Others stroll through libraries, campus coffee shops, and other gathering places. It's easy to pick up a backpack or laptop and keep walking. If you live in an apartment area that is rented mostly by students, you should realize that thieves know when students move in and that they bring computers, smart phones, TVs, and cash. It can be easy to dash into an unlocked room or apartment, grab a laptop or wallet off of a desk, and then walk away looking like any other student. You should always be diligent locking your doors and keeping track of your belongings.

The other high-crime moment is on the street after dark, particularly late at night. Being alone on the street late at night may not be safe, whether you're a man or a woman. If you're a woman, there's also the greater likelihood that you may be the victim of a sexual assault. You should check to see if your community college has a "safe walk" program you can call for someone to walk you to your car if you have night classes or stay late at the library. You should know the location of the campus emergency phones that connect directly to the campus security and immediately notify them of your location. Always make sure your cell phone is quickly accessible.

Respect yourself enough not to put yourself in dangerous situations. Take simple steps to minimize the odds of becoming a crime victim.

6. Avoid Dangerous Situations and Get Help in Emergencies

The first rule of safety is that you should not put yourself in a situation that has a high potential to endanger you and others. The second rule is to have an exit strategy if you should find yourself in a difficult or dangerous situation. Why do you need this second rule if you follow the first rule? The reason is that you can't always fully control your circumstances, try as you might. Sometimes, through no fault of your own, you may find yourself in a potentially dangerous situation.

To have an exit strategy, you need to imagine what might happen. If you have night classes or work late at the library, imagine what you would do if you encountered threatening people. Is your cell phone programmed with the number for campus security? Do you know where the campus emergency phones are?

Imagine what you would do if the friend who drove you to a party is too drunk to drive and won't let you drive home. You always have your cell phone, but did you remember to bring enough money to get a taxi? Imagine what you would do if, on a date, things move along faster than you have anticipated. Have you remembered to bring protection? Are you prepared to talk with your partner about protection or to stop?

Despite all your precautions, it is possible that an emergency situation may occur while you're attending college. Although you may have always depended on others—parents or spouses—to respond in the event of emergencies, you should now be prepared to take action if emergencies arise—whether they involve you or others.

One emergency situation that occurs among young adults with some frequency is alcohol poisoning. Someone goes to a party, drinks far more than he or she can handle, and collapses. It is essential that you call 9-1-1 immediately. We have heard of students hesitating to call 9-1-1 because they feared, rightfully or wrongfully, that the police would ticket them or their friend for being a minor in possession of alcohol. In the meantime, the friend lost precious minutes of urgently needed medical attention. If you find yourself in this situation, call 9-1-1 and get help immediately!

Another type of emergency situation involves a sexual assault. If you—or a friend—have been sexually assaulted, get help. Medical, counseling, and criminal issues may be involved that need to be addressed. Most campus security and city police today have officers who are specially trained to respond sensitively and thoroughly with individuals who are victims of sexual assault. The same is true at most hospital emergency rooms.

You may know a student who has a medical or psychiatric emergency. If you come upon a student who has collapsed, is having difficulty breathing, or is wounded and bleeding, immediately call 9-1-1 for emergency medical attention. If this were to happen to you, is your cell phone programmed so that emergency department personnel would know who to contact?

There are other kinds of emergencies as well, for instance, students who have stopped taking medications for physical or psychiatric disorders or ones whose dramatic weight loss suggests problems with an eating disorder. These kinds of emergency situations can often have some impact on a student's academic progress, even if it is short term. Encourage the student to contact his or her advisor or the Dean of Student Services, or do so yourself. If the student cannot attend class, these administrators will alert the instructor that there is a legitimate reason why this student is not in class or will be turning in exams or assignments late. When the immediate emergency has passed, the student can then follow up with each individual instructor to make whatever additional arrangements might be necessary.

Dealing with an emergency may be frightening, especially the first time. You should feel confident, however, that community college officials, medical and counseling staffs, and police officers are all well prepared for such situations and are there to help you out. They have considerable experience with these situations and will provide guidance on how to deal with the immediate emergency and any necessary follow-up.

7. Learn about and Use Health and Counseling Services

All community colleges have invaluable resources available to support student well-being. Take full advantage of these resources and services because they will serve you well. Especially if your tuition and fees pay for these services, you shouldn't hesitate for even a second.

If your college has a health center, you should definitely consider it one of your valuable resources. If your college does not have a health center, staff or faculty in the student services and/or student life offices may be able to provide you with referrals to community services. There are many reasons you might choose to visit the health center. The most obvious reason would be if you're ill or injured—if you have a fever, a sore throat, a sprained ankle, or stomach flu. Go to the college or community health center to see a doctor or nurse.

You might also want to visit a health center if you need birth control devices, think you might be pregnant, or want to be tested for sexually transmitted diseases. You may come to college with previously diagnosed problems and need continuing treatment of headaches, eating disorders, vision problems, or depression.

Most community colleges do have a counseling center or can refer you to free or low-cost services in the community. At counseling centers, on-staff counselors schedule regular appointments, but most also have walk-in hours when you can just drop in without an appointment and someone will be available to see you. Several decades ago there was a stigma attached to seeing a counselor or therapist, but today quite the opposite is true.

Students go to the counseling center for a variety of reasons. You might be very homesick or might have a close relative at home who is not well and you want to talk to someone about the situation. You might find that you are having trouble adjusting to going to the community college or being on your own for the first time. Family members might be having health or marital problems or financial difficulties. You might find yourself in a relationship that is breaking up badly, or you might be in a relationship with a person who is manipulative and abusive.

Sometimes, when students have academic problems, the cause may lie with issues that are not related to the classroom but need to be addressed in the counseling center. Some students have problems managing their money for the first time, and they need to talk with someone about how to get those issues, like credit card abuse, under better control.

If a student is sexually assaulted while on campus, the counseling center and health center are there to help. Some students abuse drugs or are alcoholic, and when they are ready to seek help, they may get coordinated support from both the counseling center and health center. Still other students are suicidal, and the counseling center can help them address that issue.

Whatever services are available on campus or in your community, you should take full advantage of them. If you're in doubt about whether your problem is serious enough to go to the health or counseling center, by all means err on the side of going for help. Getting routine help and support for your physical and emotional/mental health is an important factor in your academic success and your ability to achieve your goals.

9

Look Beyond the First Year of Community College

1. Explore Possible Majors

If you are attending community college as preparation for transfer to a four-year school, you may be asked when you apply to transfer whether you have completed the prerequisites for your major or concentration. This means that, in addition to completing your general university requirements, you will need to have decided on a major. Some students come into community college very certain about what they want to study. Many, however, come to community college wanting to explore a wide range of subject areas and topics and are undecided about a major.

Students who have already decided their field of study prior to coming to community college may already be taking the required courses for their majors, such as art, engineering, or nursing. Even within these fields, however, students will need to make decisions about subfields of study during their undergraduate years.

Another group of students who often appear certain about their choice of major are those who are considered preprofessional. Students who plan to attend law school often major in political science, and those interested in a career in business often choose economics. These students limit their choice of majors as a result of the widespread myth that it's essential to have those particular majors in order to gain admission to law or business school, respectively. That is simply not the case. Choose a major in a field that you find stimulating, not one that holds little or no interest for you.

Students planning to apply to medical school are required to complete many prerequisites during their undergraduate studies. Unlike their preprofessional peers in law and business, many of these highly competitive students feel pressured to double- or triple-major in order to look good on their medical school applications, so they choose to major in a science discipline like biology as well as a discipline in the social sciences or humanities. It's not necessary for you to double-major, but at least for these more narrowly focused students, this choice allows them to get a broader liberal arts education.

Most students arrive at community college undecided about their major. Most high school curricula, and indeed, most jobs, provide little opportunity to even begin to imagine the vast world of ideas and fields of study. Both preprofessional and undecided students are well known for changing their minds about their major multiple times during their community college careers. Don't think of that as a problem. It's a natural step in the decision-making process as you take intriguing courses in new fields and then begin to pursue those subject areas in greater depth.

2. Check Out Your Community College Employment and Career Center

Whether you are certain about your major or undecided, in a professional-technical program, or planning to transfer to a four-year college or university, you will definitely want to visit the employment and career center at your community college if available. Even if you plan to transfer to a four-year college, you will want and need to work to support yourself. You will want to take advantage of the wealth of resources that can help you make informed choices as you progress toward your goals.

If you are a transfer student and are undecided about a major, there are academic advisors who can help you puzzle out your choices. They are skilled at helping you think through your own interests and strengths and at directing you to resources that can help you understand how you can use your major once you graduate. They can help you assess your choices for transfer colleges and decide which courses you should take to help you reach your goals.

If you are considering transferring to a four-year college, carefully investigate the course and grade requirements for transfer students. Look into guaranteed admissions programs available in some states. Pay close attention to the strict guidelines.

No matter what your educational goals are—completing an occupational program or ultimately earning a four-year degree—staff in the career services office can help you to select a major or career path. Most have a library of resources (books, magazines, videos, and Internet links) so that you can research various occupational fields and the labor market. Check out the workshops that they offer on job search tips, guidance in how to write effective resumes and cover letters, and suggestions for, and even practice in, preparing for job interviews. You should also check out their programs for helping students connect with potential employers. This might include mentoring programs, job fairs, and networking services. They might also have job listings and offer job referrals for students and alumni.

Finally, while you are contemplating all of this information to help you with your future, don't forget to take advantage of the information that can help you now. Check out the employment possibilities for students, including work-study positions both on and off campus and cooperative education positions for students in professional-technical degree programs.

3. If Necessary, Look into Transferring to Another College

You may find that you are one of those students who wants or needs to change schools after one or two terms. Any number of reasons might require you to consider transferring to a different community college. Examine this possibility carefully, thoughtfully, and dispassionately so that you make the best decision, and be sure to keep your options open as you begin the process of applying to other schools. If you are looking to transfer to a for-profit college, examine it carefully for information on accreditation, and look deeply and carefully at information about costs.

There are many reasons students consider transferring. You may find that the community college you are attending is not the right fit for you. Some students want a community college that has more opportunities in the arts, music, or sports, or a program in a specialized field like dental hygiene or environmental technology.

Changes in your family through death, illness, divorce, or a job loss may also require a move to a different community college. Some students may decide they wish to live further from their parent(s) or closer to a partner they see as a future spouse. Some community colleges may not have adequate childcare or may not be hospitable to students who work all day and need to take evening courses. Other students dislike a particular community college's size (too large or too small) or environment (urban or rural). Some minority students find a particular campus climate inhospitable, and others dislike the lack of diversity.

Before transferring, however, you should be sure that your feeling is persistent, that your unhappiness is not a reaction to one particular incident or event, such as a low grade on a test, an instructor's critical comments in class, or not getting a lead role in a play. These circumstances and others like them can make you feel like you're not wanted at this community college. However, you want to ascertain whether they are indicative of a campus culture that is not a good fit for you overall or whether you will be able to get past these unhappy moments to enjoy all that is good about the environment.

Transferring to another college, whether it is a community, technical, or four-year college, is a perfectly reasonable option, but don't act quickly. It can be a good and necessary choice for you, but take your time to decide. You can apply to transfer to other community colleges without dropping out of your current school. That will buy you time to see if the negative impressions and difficult circumstances persist throughout the school year.

Whatever college(s) you attend as you pursue your degree, you want to have a rewarding and fulfilling experience. Be sure changing colleges will help you achieve that goal.

4. Turn Slumps into Opportunities

It happens, and it is for real. Your first terms at college are an adrenaline rush, filled with new courses, new people, new activities, and a tremendous surge of excitement about new knowledge and opportunities.

In subsequent terms, most students expect the rush to continue to carry them, just like it did during the first terms. The problem is that eventually the rush dissipates, your energy dwindles, and the forward thrust of your experience slows down, often dramatically. It's not that anything negative takes place, just that eventually the surge of excitement of all the newness begins to wear off.

The challenge is to learn from all your experiences and to take control and responsibility for your choices, academic and otherwise. The rush of the first term must now be transformed into intrinsic motivation and commitment about your choices. The excitement and enthusiasm that reflected your adrenaline rush must now be sustained as part of your continuing approach to academics, social experiences, and the changes you have decided to make in your life.

The slump does happen to many students; it's not a myth. For some it will come earlier, and for others it'll come later when they are close to completing their degree. You may feel good about everything but just more sluggish. You may still like all the courses you're taking but find it's harder to do all the reading. You may begin to think that your part-time job at the tattoo parlor isn't so bad after all or that you were crazy to think it would be worth so much time, effort, and money to earn a degree. Maybe taking courses that are required for your program or major seems like too much drudgery.

We don't know if you can avoid slumps altogether, but you can certainly minimize the experience. The first step is for you to acknowledge the likelihood that you will experience a slump at some point. The second step is to identify those practices that were most meaningful to you when you began and, if necessary, to plan for some new challenges and experiences.

What new challenges might you take on? You might decide to take on a leadership role in a campus organization to further develop your skills. You could look forward to a new living situation or to expanding your current group of friends. You might look forward to taking some new courses, either because you've completed the necessary prerequisites or because you now know which are the best instructors and you want to study with them. Maybe what you need to do is play a sport or pick up a musical instrument or regroup and reflect on your long-range plans. What do you want to be doing in three, five, or ten years? What steps are worth taking to help you reach that goal?

All of these choices take you a step beyond your initial experiences, presenting you with new and stimulating personal, social, and intellectual challenges and the chance to remember that you have taken control and responsibility for your education and life path to an extent that you couldn't have imagined just a few years ago. This is no slump; you're living a great life.

5. Work Steadily toward Your Timely Graduation

Community college is a great experience, a chance to explore your potential and your interests. However, you will want to find the right balance between taking too long and rushing to complete.

There are certainly many good reasons why it may take more than two years to complete your degree. One reason is financial need, which can force you to attend part-time or to postpone your education because you cannot afford to pay for school expenses. A second reason is that you are working or supporting a family and cannot afford, financially or in terms of time, to attend school full time. A third good reason is that you or family members have health problems that require you to care for yourself or others. A fourth good reason is that you change your major and require additional time to complete your degree or preprofessional requirements. A fifth good reason is that you need to review some skills like math, reading, or writing in order to be fully prepared for the demands of college level work.

Some students are delayed in their progress toward their degree because their community college does not offer a sufficient number of courses in required fields each term to allow all interested students to complete their degree requirements in a timely fashion. If this is your situation, the best strategy is to work closely with your academic advisor to develop a plan, one that ensures that you are prepared to enroll in the courses that you need when they are offered.

If, on the other hand, you took too many credits or experienced a challenging term that resulted in low grades or the need to withdraw, an advisor can help you figure out what happened and develop a plan that helps you move toward achieving your goals.

Some students transfer to a four-year college without completing their AA or AS degree. If you need only one or two more courses to complete your degree, consider carefully whether it's in your best interest to finish the AA or AS degree while still moving forward with the transfer.

Some students are unsure of a career path or major or change their majors one or more times. That's fine; it's not a problem. In fact, it can be one of the best decisions you make. However, if you are in this situation, you should explore your interests and abilities. If your community college offers courses or workshops in career exploration, take advantage of them. You should keep in mind, however, that many programs and majors have very specific requirements. Working closely with an academic advisor can help you make careful choices about your coursework as you explore possible fields of interest.

Sometimes you will find that the key to the puzzle of discovering a compelling direction will be found more easily outside of community college. If you haven't found your way in the first year, you could begin exploring unfinished questions outside of the college arena. You may want to take time off to travel, work at different types of jobs, or get on-the-job training. Within a year or two, you should have a better idea of what field interests you and what you want to pursue as you complete your community college degree.

Set a realistic goal for completion of your degree, and focus your efforts on realizing all the benefits of community college within that time frame. Be attentive to course requirements and consult regularly with an academic advisor. You may have good reason to extend your education beyond your planned timeline, and you shouldn't stress about doing so. But to the extent that you have control over matters, progress deliberately and successfully toward your goals. There are great things ahead of you beyond community college.

6. Ask for Letters of Recommendation

Every job, internship, and four-year transfer college will ask you to provide references. After you're in community college, it will no longer be good enough to get a letter from your favorite high school teacher, the manager of the store where you worked, your clergy-person, or a friend of the family who has seen you grow up and flourish.

Instructors at your community college will be the most important source of letters of recommendation for you during your college years and beyond. You may find that you need these letters as early as your first term or year or the beginning of your second year of college. If you are looking for a summer internship, a research assistantship, acceptance to a study abroad program, or a job in the library, you will be asked to provide a letter from an instructor on campus.

Later, when you apply to transfer, it is critical that you can turn to at least two or three faculty members who will write outstanding letters on your behalf.

Most instructors will be more than willing to write one or even multiple letters for you, but only if you have developed a relationship with them or have caught their attention through your comments in class discussion, by writing an exceptional paper, or by visiting during office hours.

A small number of very special instructors, usually those who have been so impressed with you that they are willing to serve as your advocates, will go out of their way and initiate calls and contacts on your behalf. They will keep you in mind when they hear of scholarship opportunities, summer internships, and special study programs. They will make it their business to help you get into the four-year college of your choice.

Some instructors will be willing to write letters but will not be reliable about deadlines. You need to keep tabs on whether the letters you have requested have been submitted in a timely manner. If you can't depend on someone to write a letter for you on time, you should find a replacement.

When you do ask for a letter, you want to make the process as easy as possible for the letter writer. If you like this professor so much that you are asking for a reference letter, it's likely that many other students are as well, and your letter is just one of several that the instructor is writing. Tell your instructor what jobs, programs, or schools you are applying to and give him or her a copy of your resume, any forms that need to be filled out (usually you will have to complete part of the forms), a short written reminder about the purpose of the letter, and the due date. If it's possible to send the letter via email or through a website, ask your instructor if he or she would prefer to send a letter this way or by snail mail. If the latter, include a stamped, addressed envelope for the instructor to use. Let your instructor know the eventual outcome of your applications; he or she will be interested to hear.

The key to asking for reference letters is to know instructors well enough that you can approach them. Your first task in securing references is building your relationships with your instructors. After you've done that, don't be shy about asking for letters. Instructors will be pleased and honored that you have asked and will be eager to learn that you have succeeded in your job search or pursuit of academic and professional degrees.

7. Keep Good Records and Plan for Completion

Once in a while students will come to an advising session without knowing which courses they have taken or, even worse, which ones they are enrolled in at the time. We recognize how busy life can be, but it is critically important to begin the process of keeping very good records of your work and your progress toward your goals.

You will always want to be completely prepared for your meetings with your academic advisor. The first reason, of course, is so that you don't waste valuable time—yours and your advisor's—looking up information. You also want to convey how serious you are about your community college work and your plans for your own future.

You should establish a system for keeping track of your community college work. You can do this electronically or in print form. Some of our students show up to advising sessions with their laptops and the files with their records easily accessible. Others come with a notebook or file folder neatly organized with their information. Both methods work. Both allow us to accomplish much more in our advising sessions than if we are spending our time trying to locate information.

What should you include? For starters, if you have taken placement tests in math or English, for example, you should keep a copy of the test scores and placement levels. You should include your current course enrollment and most recent college community transcript. You should also have records of any other college credits you have earned, including transcripts of coursework at other colleges as well as credit for Advanced Placement (AP) courses or programs like College in the High School. If you are enrolled in a particular program, degree track, or program for a certificate, license, or credential, you should bring any information that you have about course and degree requirements and prerequisites.

As you progress through your community college, you will begin to explore various majors, careers, and possible four-year colleges you would like to attend. Your academic advisor can help you with this, but you will need to take responsibility for some of this research yourself. For instance, if you are planning to transfer to a four-year college, you will need to explore requirements for admission to the college as well as to specific programs at the college. Some universities have more than one procedure for admission, for instance, one process for admission to the university itself and a separate one for admission to a particular undergraduate degree program like education or forestry. You will want to have a section in your records for the research you have done in this area: admission criteria, prerequisites for the major, specifics about the programs that interest you. That will allow you to talk with your advisor about which choices work best for you.

You should also keep a checklist of steps you will need to take to complete your degree. Sometimes students think that simply completing a specified number of credits will automatically lead to a degree. However, most community colleges not only have degree requirements, they have steps for completion. You will want to know how to apply for graduation and a transcript evaluation and the deadline at your community college for doing so.

You should also have a place where you keep course syllabi and graded, completed coursework. Sometimes former students contact us, asking for a copy of the syllabus from a course they took from us years ago. Having decided to return to school or to apply to a four-year college, they discover that course numbers and titles vary from college to college and in different states, and to prove they have met the requirements for their program, they need to provide a syllabus. Also, some universities require that students complete and submit portfolios of their coursework—papers, projects, artwork, presentations—and faculty evaluation of those. These might be for admission into a program or part of the degree completion requirements. You should not expect that your instructors have the space to store all of the coursework completed by their students. Remember to pick up your work at the end of the term and to store it in a safe place.

While it may seem unnecessary or time-consuming to take these steps now, they will save you valuable time later. Plans change. Life throws curves. You should be prepared.

8. Keep Track of Your Accomplishments

Whether you are planning to seek employment immediately after graduation or to transfer to a four-year school, you should consider keeping a good record of your accomplishments. It is not just enough to keep a list of courses you have completed. A transcript doesn't tell prospective employers and transfer universities all that you have been doing and all that you can do with what you have learned.

You will have numerous accomplishments, large and small, during your community college years. Be sure to make a note of them in a journal, in a file, in a video, or on your resume. If you're not the kind of person who keeps good files, then make sure at the very least that you keep a list of your accomplishments. Time will go by so quickly that unless you have an intentional, organized system for keeping memories, you will lose track of so much good that you have done.

Some of your accomplishments will be in the academic arena. You may get comments from an instructor expressing what an outstanding exam or paper you've written. Keep that paper and hold onto those special words. You may be more formally recognized by being placed on the college honor roll or acknowledged at a college honors ceremony. You might be invited to serve on a college policy committee or to give input into departmental curricular projects. You may win a prize for poetry, participate on the debate team, star in a theatrical performance, exhibit artwork, or be invited to present the results of a research paper or project to a community group.

Other accomplishments will be based on your personal and community achievements. You may win a scholarship for civic involvement, be elected or appointed to a leadership position in an organization, or get a promotion at your workplace. You might play in the school's marching band, make the varsity gymnastics team, or score the winning goal in an intramural game. Keep a file of all these accomplishments. Someone you admire may say something very complimentary about you; write in a journal how you felt.

At some point, you should begin to think about how all of your community college experience ties together. Try listing how your accomplishments add up in your perspective. What skills have you developed as a result of all these experiences? In what ways have you put your knowledge to use? Don't be nervous about doing this. You should be proud of what you have done and the recognition you receive. You don't need to feel you're gloating to feel good about yourself. Instead, imagine that you are going to convince an employer or transfer college why you are the person they should select.

Finally, no matter what your future plans, you should do this for yourself. When you begin community college, it will seem like you have an endless road ahead of you. However, at some point in the future, you will feel that the experience went by very quickly. Hold onto your best memories, even as you continue to create special, new ones each and every day.